The Only

Retirement Planning Book

You'll Ever Need

Your Guide To a Stress-Free Retirement: Achieve
Financial Freedom. Make Your Money Last,
& Savor Life After Work

By

Garrett Monroe

Contents

Your Guide to a Stress-Free Retirement

When you think about retirement, do you envision:

- Traveling in an RV with a little dog?

- Summering in the south and wintering in the north?

- Moving closer to the kids or grandkids?

- Spending time at a house on the lake tossing a fishing pole into the water?

- Nothing, other than freedom from the 9-to-5 grind, the commute, and your boss?

Whatever your goals, one thing is clear: It's going to take a bit of planning to ensure that you have what you need to do what you want.

Many people reach retirement age and think they'll be able to rely on social security. Or, if they've planned ahead, they religiously put their money into a 401(k) plan and assumed that it would grow into a large nest egg.

Others find themselves nearing age 50 and starting to panic, falling for get-rich-quick schemes, hoping they can "catch up" with extra deductions, making risky choices in their mutual fund by "playing the market," or resigning themselves to the fact that they're going to have to work until they're 90.

Historically, we've been taught that if we start saving in our 20s and choose a well-balanced mutual fund, we'll be fine by the time we retire. But what about those of us who didn't choose a corporate job, borrowed money from the fund to pay some bills along the way, and reached retirement age without much advisement?

Too many folks who've already retired—or *thought* that they'd retired—have headed back to the workplace just to make ends meet. Alternatively, they're faced with unexpected health problems that either put a dent in their funds or a kink in their hopeful plans for the future.

Then there's the aspect of change—in other words, how to adjust going from a 40-hour work week and commute to being at home full time or in an RV park. It's understatement that retirement planning isn't just about money.

If you're facing these or similar questions about what life will look like after retirement, you've got the right book in your hands. Throughout these pages, **you'll discover ways to determine:**

- The amount of money you need to live the life you want

- Strategies to make your money work for you—before and during retirement

- What to do if you find yourself short on funds

- How to set retirement goals with your money, lifestyle, health, and legacy

- How to sift through the myriad of financial-planning accounts to determine the right one for your goals

- Ways to save money on taxes

- How to choose investments within your retirement account

- How to stay sharp during your post-working existence through taking care of your health, building social connections, and keeping your mind sharp

- Where and how to get extra help when you need it

And rest assured—this information is factual, reliable, and drawn from a wealth experience. Under the pen name Garrett Monroe, we're a team of writers with varied business experience from multiple industries, including retirement planning, sales, real estate, coaching, and accounting. We've pooled our extensive experience to assist you in achieving a fulfilling retirement—the one you desire and the one you deserve.

Ask yourself the following. Do you feel:

- That you won't have enough money to be able to retire comfortably (or at all)?

- That since you didn't start saving at 21 you'll struggle in your retirement years?

- That you don't know enough to make sound decisions about retirement?

Thinking about retirement shouldn't send you into panic mode about whether or not you're prepared for it. But simply by picking up this book, you've taken a solid step in deciding that you don't want to leave your retirement future to chance. And that's an excellent starting point.

The Only Retirement Book You'll Ever Need is designed to alleviate stress and give you concrete tools that'll have you easing into retirement with a well-thought-out plan. Think of us as your trusted advisors, helping you to set up a blueprint for success.

We'll start with the basics and introduce you to the tips and strategies we've discovered while researching and setting up our own retirement plans. But this book accomplishes much more than that. We know that your situation is unique, so whether you're in your 20s and maximizing your retirement contributions, in your 50s and finding yourself in catch-up mode, or in your 70s and thinking about legacy planning, this guide will absolutely help you. By the end, you'll feel more than confident about your retirement plans going forward, and then you can get back to the fun stuff—like living life to the fullest in the meantime. Let's get started on building and planning a life-after-work that you're excited (and not stressed in the slightest) about.

Chapter 1

Laying a Solid Foundation for Your Ultimate Retirement

"I see retirement as just another of these reinventions, another chance to do new things and be a new version of myself."

-Walt Mossberg, former technology columnist for The Wall Street Journal

Retirement 101: More Than Just a Long Vacation

Retirement means more than just "not working"—it's about enjoying the well-earned fruits of your labor. You've paid your dues as a productive member of society, and now you get to enjoy your golden years. Retirement signals the end of one phase of your life and the start of another, and it's your chance to relax with loved ones or pursue the passions that you've always dreamed of. Instead of competing on the weekends for space on the green, you can head to the golf course on a Tuesday, hit the hiking trails on Thursday, or sleep in late on Monday. Or maybe even all those things. Who's stopping you?

That said, to make the most out of retirement, you must approach it carefully. This not only includes the financial aspect, but also healthcare, social connections, estate planning, and keeping your mind and body active. So many of us tie our identities to their jobs, and when the time comes to move on, we often have a tough time of it. Consider the 65-year-old woman working in the bakery at the grocery store. Without knowing her story, you might feel sorry for her that she has to work to pay bills, but the reality might be that she feels lost without her job.

If you, too, imagine that you might feel set adrift without a sail after retiring, spend some time reflecting on your interests. What hobbies did you never have time for? Consider contacting a local senior center to see what activities they have to offer—computer programming, mentoring youth, classes, and luncheons are just a few of the many activities you can check out. The American Association of Retired Persons (AARP) is a well-known organization with plenty of resources and discounts for those of us over 50. [1]

Here's the reality: Your choices after retirement will likely be limited by how well you've prepared. If you'd love to stay in your home but have a mortgage payment that's beyond your means, you may face some tough decisions.

But before you panic, let's dig into the facts.

What Retirement Really Means (Hint: It's Not Just Bingo)

Hey—we have nothing against bingo. If you love the game, by all means, knock yourself out! Bingo halls are a great place to meet up with friends and test your luck. But generally, Bingo isn't an everyday thing, and even if it was, it might not be *your* thing. So it's important to find out what to do the rest of the time you suddenly find yourself with.

Retirement can involve personal growth, lifestyle adjustments, and the pursuit of newfound passions—all of which look different for everyone. Some people, when they find themselves with extra time, like to take long hikes in the woods to look for birds, while others enjoy curling up on a chair and reading a book.

Some might rediscover a hobby they never had the time for, and some might find fulfillment in a volunteer opportunity.

The point is that retirement isn't "one size fits all"—not in the slightest. In fact, we know of someone who retired and was so bored that he ended up going back to work. Incredulously, he's almost 90, and we're not sure *what* he'd do if he had to stay home all day. Another friend is in his 60s and embarking on a new business. When asked about retirement, his response was "This *is* my retirement." Someone else we know has a simple part-time job and travels to Mexico for golf vacations several times a year. And another friend moved to a house on a lake and spends her time volunteering at a local organization.

Each of their retirement plans look very different from one another, and so will yours (unless, of course, you'd like to copy one of their ideas—in which case, go for it!).

Why Planning Ahead Is Crucial for Your Golden Years

For those of you who chose a traditional working path, you may have gone to work for a company in your 20s and, now that you've put in 30-35 years, you've decided that it's time to stop working. Your office threw you a big retirement bash and you walked out the door with an engraved plaque, as well as the box of pictures and mementos that had been sitting on your desk. One day you're heading to the office and the next day you're not. Or perhaps you decided to set off on a celebratory cruise, but then you transitioned into a new version of daily life. You start drawing from your retirement plan, live off of your savings, and, depending on your age, start collecting social security.

If you had multiple jobs or were self-employed throughout your career, you might have an individual retirement account. And if you worked for the government, you might have a pension.

Whichever way you get (or got) there, you have a set amount of money to start with (but you can also continue to grow money in mutual funds, savings accounts, and other investment options). However, you do need to consider taxes on your distributions, so if you're not savvy with numbers, check with a financial advisor.

In general, planning ahead makes things easier by allowing you to:

- Build a solid financial foundation for retirement. You can accumulate the funds needed to maintain your desired lifestyle and cover potential healthcare costs.

- Pay off debts before retirement, build a nest egg, and determine which goals you can realistically achieve.

- Take advantage of the power of compound interest, creating passive income.

- Adapt to potential lifestyle changes, including downsizing your home and adjusting spending habits based on your new income.

- Prepare for potential health concerns and medical expenses.

- Decide how your assets will be distributed to your family members or to charities.

- Spend time in retirement enjoying life instead of worrying about the details of how you're going to pay for it.

How Age Affects Retirement Planning

It's common sense that the earlier you start to save, the more time you have to build up retirement savings. Below is an ideal breakdown of how retirement planning can be addressed in different decades of your life.

In your 20s and 30s:

- You can take advantage of compounding interest, meaning that as your portfolio grows, you earn interest on an ever-increasing balance.

- You have a higher tolerance for risk. There's more time for your portfolio to rebound if the market hits a slump.

- You can build effective savings habits that'll last a lifetime.

In your 40s and 50s:

- You're somewhere around the middle of your career. Perhaps you've received some raises or promotions and may be in your peak earning years.

- You can start to think about what retirement will look like for you.

- You can diversify your portfolio with a mix of slow and steady earning funds, as well as some risk.

- You can take advantage of catch-up contributions (after you turn 50), which allow you to set aside more money to reach your retirement goals.

In your late 50s to early 60s:

- You're really starting to think about retirement and looking to see what your portfolio will allow you to do or what changes you might need to consider.

- You can investigate how much Social Security will add to your income. Remember—the longer you delay starting these payments, the higher the monthly check might be.

- You can check out healthcare options as well, perhaps by looking into long-term care insurance.

- It's time to review and update your estate plan and determine where your retirement funds will go if you don't use them all up.

In your 60s (and beyond):

- You're taking care of your health and wellness to ensure that you can enjoy your retirement years. If you live to be 80 or 90 (or even longer), can you provide for your care?

- You're developing a systematic withdrawal strategy to sustain your income throughout retirement.

- You're mindful enough to reevaluate your plans if your circumstances change or your portfolio changes with the market.

- You're preparing all the paperwork for leaving a financial legacy (if this is important for you). You're also making sure that your closest family members understand your desires.

Retirement Expectations vs. Reality

Life rarely goes as planned—this is something that all of us are keenly aware of. While many people envision a period of relaxation and enjoyment, the actual experience may be influenced by various factors. For example, **you might:**

- Expect financial freedom but unforeseen expenses could arise. We suggest an emergency fund, savings, and insurance policies for things like home repairs, new cars, or helping out a loved one.

- Plan to travel extensively but instead face health concerns, budget constraints, or unexpected circumstances (think global crisis or pandemic—we've been through both!).

- Envision time with family and friends but find that you live too far away or that they have other plans.

- Anticipate healthy living but face health challenges with yourself or a loved one. What happens if your partner becomes ill and can't participate in planned activities?

- Expect a stable financial environment but the world ends up facing economic downturns, rising prices, changes in interest rates, or inflation.

- Have every intention of staying in your home but changes in your health or the economy force you to downsize or relocate.

Many people approach retirement as a time to relax and find emotional fulfillment (especially if they lacked satisfaction in their career). If the reality is different due to family dynamics, personal choices, health issues, or another factor, you might have trouble adjusting to the circumstances. Always remember that the key traits in your retirement years are *flexibility* and *resilience*.

Setting Course: Envisioning Your Retirement Goals

Imagining what retirement might look like for you is a dynamic and ongoing process. By taking the time to reflect on your values, you can create a roadmap for a fulfilling and purposeful post-work existence. Regularly revisiting and adjusting your goals ensures that your retirement plan remains aligned with your changing goals.

Financial Goals: Making Your Money Work for You

To set yourself up for financial comfortability, consider the following some tips:

- Start by setting clear financial goals based on short-term, medium-term, and long-term needs.

- Create a budget to track your income, categorize spending, and prioritize savings.

- Establish an emergency fund equal to three to six months of living expenses to handle unforeseen situations.

- Manage debt by focusing on high-interest payments and exploring consolidation options.

- Save and invest early to benefit from compound interest, thereby diversifying investments for risk reduction.

- Prioritize contributions to retirement accounts and take advantage of employer matches.

- Stay informed about personal finance, consider professional advice for complex decisions, and regularly review and adjust your financial plan.

- Ensure that you have adequate insurance coverage.

- Practice mindful spending by distinguishing between needs and wants.

- Seek professional advice for matters like estate planning.

- Stay disciplined in following your financial plan, adapting as needed.

Remember—financial goals are personal, so customize these principles to fit your situation and then regularly reassess as life changes.

Lifestyle Goals: Your Retirement, Your Rules

Planning for retirement means creating a lifestyle that matches your vision for the future. This might include:

- Envisioning the activities, travel, and daily routines you want in your ideal retirement.

- Estimating all your retirement expenses, including healthcare, travel, and leisure activities, to figure out your financial needs.

- Considering healthcare costs and addressing high-interest debts before retiring.

- Budgeting for hobbies, travel, and downsizing, and evaluating the impact on your retirement.

- Thinking about part-time work or engaging in hobbies for extra income and social connections.

- Regularly reviewing and adjusting your retirement plan, as well as considering long-term care insurance.

- Developing an estate plan for assets and end-of-life decisions.

- Embracing retirement as an opportunity to explore new interests and enjoy life.

- Staying informed about financial news and trends, and being flexible to adapt to changes.

Proactive planning aligned with your retirement vision helps you achieve a fulfilling and freedom-filled retirement.

Health Goals: Because Wealth Is Nothing Without Health

Focusing on your physical well-being is crucial because wealth means little without good health. **The following are some key principles for a healthier lifestyle:**

- Include regular exercise, like walks or gym sessions, and adopt a balanced diet with foods that work for your body.

- Stay hydrated, get seven to nine hours of quality sleep, and manage stress through techniques like meditation.

- Regular health examinations and screenings are crucial for identifying potential issues early on.

- Avoid harmful substances like tobacco, processed foods, and excessive alcohol, prioritize mental health, and nurture positive social connections.

- Reduce sedentary behavior, set personalized health goals, and stay informed about health topics.

- Practice mindful eating, maintain hygiene, and engage in hobbies for a holistic approach. Maybe there were some hobbies that you didn't quite have time for in your working days, but with your new flexibility, you can embrace new interests.

- Manage your body weight through balanced nutrition and exercise, and develop habits for long-term health. You can even look into hiring a personal trainer to make sure that you stay consistent.

- Ensure that your finances are accompanied by the invaluable asset of good health, which can lead to more fulfilling retirement years.

Legacy Goals: Creating More Than Just Memories

Building a meaningful legacy is about making a lasting impact, and it starts by figuring out what matters to you—your core values and the goals that drive you. **Below are some ways to create more than just memories with your legacy goals:**

- Share your personal stories and lessons with those you care about, thus passing on your family values. If something is really important for you, you can even consider recording it, perhaps via a podcast or maybe just an audio file for your family to go back and listen to.

- Plan for the financial well-being of future generations by supporting education, philanthropy, and causes you believe in.

- Express your creativity and back ventures that align with your values. Be a champion for health, mentorship, and leadership development.

- Document your wisdom and align legal matters with your legacy.

- Take time to reflect on and adjust your goals as life evolves.

- Most importantly, live each day in a way that mirrors the legacy you want to leave behind.

These personal steps contribute to a meaningful legacy that leaves a positive mark on future generations.

Key Elements for Living "The Good Life"

In the end, living what everyone calls "the good life" means focusing on what truly matters. This looks different for each person and may include taking care of your health and creating meaningful relationships with your family, friends, and the community. You might also want to seek out activities that bring joy and a sense of purpose, finding that balance between work and personal life.

Other traits of "the good life" might include lifelong learning, being present in the moment, staying true to yourself, and making time for activities that bring you joy. Developing resilience, giving back, and prioritizing self-care are key aspects of daily life. Cultivating positive habits, maintaining healthy relationships with technology, and spending time in nature also play key roles.

And, of course, there's something to be said for relaxing and laying low, too. You've worked hard all your life, and you're entitled to spend your retired years exactly how you want to. This could mean traveling the world, or maybe just enjoying some quiet days at home with your family and a good Netflix show. It's your retirement and you've earned it, so ultimately, the call is yours! You just need to ensure that you have the funds to afford the lifestyle you're picturing.

Income Sources & Golden Eggs

Here, we're referring to the various ways through which you can earn money. **These include:**

- Employment income

- Income from a business you own

- Investment income such as interest, dividends, or capital gains

- Rental income

- Royalties from patents, copyrights, or trademarks in your name

- Income from part-time or freelance work

Think of income sources as different eggs in your financial basket. Relying on just one is generally risky due to economic changes. To build a secure financial foundation, consider having various sources like a job, freelance work, investments, or a side business.

Each income source can act as a "golden egg," so to speak, adding to your overall financial security. This is especially true of those sources that produce passive income, meaning that you essentially don't have to continuously expend effort to earn an income. For example, if you rent a house, your initial work is finding a renter. After that (unless something needs fixing or your tenant moves out and you need to find a new one), you're generating income passively.

Essentially, you want to set up your retirement income to live off of the golden eggs instead of dipping into the principal account.

When considering retirement planning, many people put all their eggs in one basket, relying on social security for all of their needs. Diversifying your income sources not only brings stability but also opens up opportunities for growth and wealth. Whether from your job, investments, or a side business, having multiple income sources helps create a stronger and safer financial future.

Realistic Budgeting, Realistic Expenses

When budgeting, think of it like planning your money journey. Keep it realistic by matching your spending plans with what you can afford by focusing on important things like housing, utilities, groceries, and transportation. And don't forget to save for emergencies and build a solid financial base. A practical budget is a useful tool, helping you handle money stress-free and making it easier to reach your financial goals.

Include some money for things you enjoy to balance your budget and add joy to your life. Also, if you have debts, allocate some funds to pay them off gradually. This not only improves your financial stability but also sets you on the path to financial freedom.

In addition, it's incredibly important to stay curious about personal finance. Keep learning about smart money habits, investment opportunities, and ways to make the most of your money. This ongoing financial literacy helps you make wise economic choices and adjust your budget as needed, ensuring a stable and healthy financial future.

Growing Your Money with Strategic Savings & Investments

Watching your cash flow grow by saving and investing is one of the best feelings around, **but there are some vital things to think about before getting started:**

- Start with an emergency fund for unexpected expenses.

- Consider options like stocks or real estate.

- Diversify your investments for safety.

- Save regularly for retirement, and use employer matches if available.

- Stay informed about financial markets and seek advice when needed.

- Set specific savings goals for big life events, like buying a new home.

- Make thoughtful spending choices, cut unnecessary expenses, and review your financial plan as life changes.

Through smart saving and investing, you can potentially increase your wealth over time and move closer to your financial goals.

This adaptable approach ensures that your money strategy stays effective over the long run. And that, ultimately, is the goal!

Risk Management: Protecting Your Nest Egg

Ensuring the safety of your savings is crucial, especially for things like retirement. To manage risk, spread your investments across different types to reduce the chance of losses. Regularly review and adjust your investment plan based on your comfort level and goals, and consider insurance to safeguard against unexpected events. This helps keep your savings safe and secure for the future.

Explore different types of insurance beyond health or life insurance, like disability insurance for added protection. Be cautious about potential scams and frauds, monitor your accounts, and use secure methods for transactions. Consistently contribute to your emergency fund for unforeseen expenses. These steps, combined with some essential smart planning, will help to protect your savings.

Social Security: Your Trusty Retirement Buddy

Think of Social Security as a dependable friend in your retirement journey. It serves as a valuable tool to enhance your retirement income, providing a foundation for a more financially secure and comfortable retirement.

Social Security stands as a crucial part of your retirement for several reasons:

- It offers essential financial support by providing a consistent income stream, helping retirees cover fundamental living expenses such as housing, food, and healthcare.

- Social Security acts as a safety net, mitigating the risk of financial hardship in old age, particularly for those without access to other retirement savings or pension plans.

- The system incorporates measures to adjust benefits for inflation, offering protection against the rising cost of living over time.

- Social Security benefits are provided for life, contributing to the financial security of individuals as they navigate through their extended retirement years.

- The program extends its impact beyond the primary earner by offering spousal and survivor benefits, as well as by providing financial support to spouses and dependents in various circumstances.

With nearly universal coverage, Social Security reaches a broad segment of the population, making it an accessible retirement benefit for the majority of workers in the United States. It fosters financial independence for retirees, reducing reliance on external sources of support and contributing to a more secure and stable retirement.

While Social Security may not suffice as the sole source of retirement income, it does play a pivotal role in forming a foundational layer of financial security, requiring careful consideration in conjunction with other retirement savings and investment strategies.

Consider Social Security as just one component of your overall retirement plan. It's important to supplement it with other savings and investment strategies to create a diversified and robust financial foundation for your retirement years. This comprehensive approach provides you with the best chance to enjoy a comfortable and financially sound retirement.

Decoding Social Security Benefits: What's in It for You

You may have apprehensions about relying on Social Security given the economy and the stories we hear about funds running out. While we wish that we could get out our crystal ball and tell you the future, we can say this for certain - do not rely solely on it. Every investment has risks, and by diversifying, you're putting yourself in a much better situation than counting on Social Security alone.

That said, it's important to understand Social Security benefits—after all, they're a crucial financial resource for your future.

To get the most from Social Security:

- Learn about eligibility and plan wisely. Factors such as your earnings history, the age at which you choose to claim benefits, and potential spousal benefits can all play pivotal roles in shaping the overall outcome.

- Think of it as a valuable income source (but not the only one) for a secure and comfortable retirement.

- Learn about options like full retirement age, delayed retirement credits, and spousal benefits to customize your approach to your financial situation.

By understanding the details and making smart choices, you can definitely improve your plan for your Social Security. When used wisely, it becomes a key component of a diversified retirement strategy, adding stability and predictability to your overall financial picture.

Knowing the Optimal Time to Apply

Deciding when to apply for benefits like Social Security is essential, and you need to consider factors like your age and personal situation. Also, explore guidelines to figure out the best time to apply, ensuring that you get the maximum benefits available to you. Stay informed about any rule changes for a more successful retirement plan.

For example, while you may be eligible to collect social security at age 62, waiting until age 70 increases your benefit amount. Exploring these strategies and understanding how they align with your retirement goals can help you make informed decisions.[2]

Maximizing Your Benefits to Get What You Deserve

Whether it's Social Security or other entitlements, it's so very important to understand the rules that surround them. Explore ways to get the most out of the benefits available to you. This proactive approach ensures that you not only navigate the complexities of these systems but also take advantage of potential opportunities for enhancement.

By diligently following these steps, you can guarantee that you'll receive the complete extent of what you're entitled to, thereby contributing significantly to your overall financial well-being. Staying informed about any updates or changes in policies related to these benefits is equally important, allowing you to adapt your strategies as needed and remain proactive in securing your financial future.

Preparing for Easy Pitches and Unexpected Curveballs

Hold on tight—get ready for both easy tasks and unexpected challenges in your journey toward financial security and a well-prepared retirement. It's vital to anticipate different scenarios and equip yourself with the skills to handle anything that comes your way. This proactive approach not only applies to financial planning but also extends to all aspects of life.

Developing resilience and adaptability enables you to navigate uncertainties and changes with greater ease. It allows you to diversify your skills, embrace qualities like adaptability and problem solving, and stay informed about financial developments. Being well-prepared allows you to respond confidently to unexpected situations, maintaining a sense of control and stability in both your financial and personal life.

Riding the Market Volatility Wave

Navigating the fluctuations of the market is comparable to riding a wave. Just like a surfer stays steady and flexible to ride the wave effectively, investors should adopt a similar mindset. Thinking long term is key—resist making hasty decisions based on short-term market changes. Spreading your investments across different assets helps manage risk, ensuring that you're not overly exposed to the fluctuations of a single market or asset class.

In the face of market volatility, patience and strategic thinking become valuable assets. Instead of reacting impulsively to short-term fluctuations, focus on the broader trends and your long-term financial goals. Periods of market ups and downs are natural, and by maintaining a disciplined and patient approach, you can navigate through these uncertainties with confidence. Consider consulting with financial advisors to align your investment strategy with your long-term objectives, helping you make informed decisions that contribute to your overall financial well-being.

Estate Planning: Simplifying Life for Your Loved Ones

This is a crucial step in ensuring that your loved ones face fewer challenges when organizing your affairs after you've passed. It encompasses vital decisions about how you want your assets distributed and involves appointing someone to manage these affairs if necessary. Creating a will, naming beneficiaries, and exploring trusts are significant steps within this process. By undertaking estate planning, you simplify the legal and financial aspects of your legacy, providing clarity and ease for your family during difficult times.

This thoughtful approach not only helps secure your legacy but also streamlines the transition of your assets, reducing potential conflicts among beneficiaries. Estate planning allows you to express your wishes explicitly, minimizing the likelihood of disputes and ensuring that your loved ones understand and follow your intentions. The establishment of trusts can offer added protection and efficiency in the distribution of assets, especially for complex estates or specific needs.

Planning your estate isn't just about money—it also includes sentimental items, family heirlooms, and even decisions about who'll take care of your kids. By dealing with these things now, you make things easier for your family later on. Talking to legal and financial experts can ensure that your plan is solid and reflects your wishes. Ultimately, look at estate planning as a worthwhile way to invest in your family's future and leave behind a meaningful legacy.

Key Takeaways

- Retirement requires advance planning for not only finances but also lifestyle, health, and legacy goals.

- Retirement funds can come from many different income sources, including investments, social security, rentals, side hustles, and golden eggs.

- The amount of money required for retirement is primarily determined by your specific financial goals.

- Social Security benefits depend on the age you start collecting them and your work history. However, don't rely on it as your sole nest egg when you retire.

- Be prepared and plan for the unexpected in your retirement years.

- Learn as much as you can about retirement benefits and review your long-term plan periodically.

Buyer Bonus

As a way of saying thank you for your purchase, we're offering our Retirement Planning Toolkit that includes three FREE downloads that are exclusive to our book readers!

First, the Retirement Planning Checklist, which gives you a step-by-step plan for planning the perfect retirement and making your money last. Second, the Estate Planning Checklist which shows you a step-by-step guide to getting your estate plan in order. And finally, the Retirement Tax Savings Guide, which shows you exactly how to minimize your taxes during retirement (and avoid costly mistakes!).

Inside these bonuses, you'll discover:

- A step-by-step checklist for your retirement plan, so you can maximize your savings and avoid any costly pitfalls.

- An exact checklist for each phase of the estate planning process, so you leave no stone unturned and make sure you're fully prepared to protect your heirs and leave a legacy.

- How to minimize your taxes in retirement so you can preserve wealth, maximize income, and achieve your financial goals.

To download your bonuses, you can go to MonroeMethod.com/retirement-plan **or simply scan the QR code below:**

Chapter 2

Retirement Bliss: Your Step-by-Step Roadmap

"For many, retirement is a time for personal growth, which becomes the path to greater freedom."

-Robert Delamontague, author and retirement expert

This chapter is about helping you create a roadmap for a fulfilling and relaxed retirement. It's not just about leaving the workforce—it's also about transitioning into a new phase of life filled with opportunities, self-discovery, and the joy of basking in the results of your hard work. We'll navigate through financial planning, lifestyle choices, and personal fulfillment, guiding you toward a retirement that isn't just an end of an era—it's also the beginning of a new, satisfying, and enriching stage in your life.

Deciding When to Retire

Ah, the almighty question of "when." Don't get us wrong—retirement absolutely *is* something to feel eager about, but it's also a big step, and there are some key factors that'll help you determine the right timing.

- **Financial Readiness**: Evaluate your financial situation to determine whether you have enough funds to cover your expected expenses. This includes minimizing or eliminating high-interest debts before retirement.

- **Health Considerations**: Assess your current health and consider any potential health issues that may arise in the future. Make sure you have healthcare and insurance coverage

- **Retirement Goals**: Determine what you want to do in retirement, such as travel, hobbies, volunteering, or spending more time with family.

- **Social and Emotional Readiness:** Retirement can be a major transition that affects your sense of identity and purpose.

- **Legal and Estate Planning:** Update wills, trusts, and powers of attorney.

- **Market Conditions:** The economy may affect the balance of your portfolio. If your balance is not where you'd like it to be, you might want to wait for more favorable conditions.

- **Government Benefits:** Programs like Social Security and Medicare have age requirements and if you wait until you are a little bit older, you can potentially receive a bigger monthly payment.

Early Retirement vs. Traditional Retirement

The traditional age of retirement is 65, which is considered to be when individuals become eligible to collect their full Social Security benefits. Depending on your situation, you may choose to retire sooner. Besides Social Security, several other retirement benefits pay out based on a certain age.

For example, employer-sponsored retirement plans such as 401(k) plans and pensions also pay out when you hit a certain age mark, and Medicare eligibility also begins at age 65.

Early retirees may need to rely more on personal savings, investments, and other income sources to bridge the gap between their current age and when they hit 65. In addition, waiting to dip into your retirement funds gives them more time to earn interest and grow. And if you started early, those last years of interest can be the most fruitful, thanks to the magic of compounding.

Factors That Could Influence Your Retirement Age

The age at which you choose to retire can be influenced by a variety of factors, and which can vary depending on the individual.

First, there's the aspect of financial readiness. The amount of savings, investments, and pension income you've accumulated and whether you're confident that those funds will support you and your planned lifestyle are likely the biggest factors. If your employer requires you to work until a certain age before collecting benefits, you might set your retirement date based on those. And if you have large debts, it might be best to pay those down before you retire. If not, you'll need to incorporate these into your monthly budget.

Health and wellness also come into play. If health concerns arise that affect the ability to work, you may choose (or be forced) to retire in order to take care of yourself or a loved one. If you're in fine health and anticipate a longer life expectancy, you may choose to work longer. Finally, there's career satisfaction. If you're happy in your job, you're naturally likely to work longer. If the workplace is volatile, such as in the case of downsizing, your employer may choose to offer an early retirement package.

The Impact (& Perks) of Working Longer

Remaining in the workforce for an extended period of time can, predictably, have both positive and negative impacts on various aspects of your life.

A most obvious upside is that continuing to work allows you to accumulate additional savings, potentially increasing your retirement nest egg. Plus, waiting to collect benefits can result in higher monthly payments.

A later retirement age can also ensure a smoother transition between receiving a paycheck and collecting benefits. Also, staying active in the workplace can provide an extended sense of purpose and mental stimulation. There can be a feeling of a lost sense of self for many when they retire—we often find fulfillment in our work, and a continued sense of contribution can positively impact our well-being. **Below are a few more perks of working longer:**

- You can continue developing professionally and personally, allowing you to stay current in your field.

- Workplace social connections can contribute to a sense of community and belonging.

- Some employers offer phased retirement options, allowing you to reduce your hours gradually and ease into retirement.

- Working longer allows you to defer minimum distributions from retirement accounts.

Conversely, working longer at a physically demanding, high-stress, or mentally draining job can adversely affect your health, and it might be a reason to consider retirement sooner rather than later.

Let's take John, for example. John is 65 years old and has worked as a correctional officer at the state prison for 40 years. He's also got a stand-up comedy business on the side, in which he books comedians and performs a bit himself, mostly as a hobby but also to make some extra money.

He could work five more years, which would add a bit more to his pension payout and leave some extra money in the bank. But each year working as a correctional officer gets more and more mentally taxing and physically draining. So John chooses to bow out and retire at 65 to enjoy his free time and put more focus into his comedy business.

This turns out to be a great decision for him. If we flash forward five years, we see some of his correctional officer colleagues who kept working, and their health and well-being have taken a big hit. Meanwhile, John has been able to pour more time into his comedy business, and he has plenty of time to recharge and relax. For John, retiring at 65 ended up being a great choice.

However, if you've got a job that isn't as mentally and physically taxing—and it's something that you love—it might be a sound decision to work a little bit longer, or at least continue on part-time for a while. It all comes down to a balancing act between whether your mental health will tolerate a few more additional years of the grind and whether you'll have the financial security to retire without worry.

Crunching the Numbers: How Much Money Will You Need?

The burning question that's asked quite often is, understandably, just how much money will you need to retire? Is $1 million in your retirement account enough? Well, your retirement is yours alone—we don't have a magic formula to predict your future, but we *can* offer up some general rules of thumb when planning.

Estimating Your Retirement Expenses

The first step in determining how much you'll need for retirement is to take a look at your current monthly expenses. This should include everything from housing costs and utilities to groceries, transportation, healthcare, and entertainment. Differentiate non-discretionary expenses, or essential costs, such as housing and healthcare from discretionary expenses, such as dining out, travel, and hobbies. You want enough to cover both, but if necessary, you also want a picture of where you could possibly make budget cuts if you needed to.

Look at your budget and consider what expenses might change in retirement. For example, perhaps you work in construction and drive a large work truck each day in order to transport supplies. During retirement, you may consider replacing that truck with something more practical for your new lifestyle. If you're close to paying off your mortgage and are planning on staying in your current house, that expense will change as well. Alternatively, you might budget more for meals at home, expenses related to your hobbies, or a new motorhome.

Also, and this is key: Be sure to factor in inflation, as the cost of living and goods is bound to rise. If your income remains steady, your dollar may not stretch as far in the future as it does now.

The 4% Rule

This is a widely used guideline in retirement planning that suggests a safe, annual withdrawal rate from retirement savings to ensure that the money lasts throughout a 30-year retirement. The 4% rule originated from a study known as the "Trinity Study," which analyzed historical market data to determine a sustainable withdrawal rate for retirees.

Here's how the 4% rule works:

- In year one, withdraw 4% of your retirement savings.

- For each subsequent year, withdraw the same amount as year one *plus* a little bit more to account for inflation.

This rule assumes that your portfolio of investments is evenly distributed among stocks and bonds.

It's important to note that the 4% rule is a guideline, not a guarantee. The success of this strategy can be influenced by individual circumstances, market conditions, and various other factors. Nevertheless, it serves as a valuable starting point when determining the longevity of your finances. It's a solid idea to work with a financial advisor who can look at your budget and savings to determine if the 4% rule will work for your specific situation, goals, and anticipated market conditions.

Inflation—The Silent Money Eater

Inflation often earns this ominous nickname because it erodes the purchasing power of money over time (refer to an inflation calendar to get historic and current rates[3]). As the prices of goods and services rise, the purchasing power of each dollar diminishes compared to its previous value. This has significant implications for retirement planning, and factoring in inflation is crucial to ensure that your income and savings remain sufficient to cover your expenses throughout your retirement. **Let's look at some key points to consider:**

- Inflation is often felt over the long term, and its effects become more pronounced over an extended retirement period. Even at a moderate inflation rate, the cost of living can significantly increase over several decades. For example, $100 in the year 2000 was worth just $56.59 in 2022, a 43.4% loss in purchasing power over just 20 years.

- Inflation *will* affect your budget. Almost certainly, most things will rise in price over time.

- Check to see if your investments have cost of living adjustments. If not, build some cushion into your budget.

- Review your investment strategy to ensure that it outpaces inflation. Consider maintaining a diversified investment portfolio that includes assets with growth potential to help protect against the eroding effects of inflation.

- When evaluating returns, use what are called "real returns." For example, if your investment generates a nominal return of 7% and inflation is 3%, the real return is 4%.

- Note that healthcare costs often rise at a rate higher than inflation, which will likely cost you more and more as you age.

- Regularly review your budget and assets to ensure that you're on track.

Budgeting for Unexpected Expenses

No matter how carefully you plan and budget, there will likely be expenses that you absolutely didn't plan for, such as medical emergencies, car and home repairs, or a job loss. Having an emergency fund gives you peace of mind. A good rule of thumb is to have three to six months' worth of living expenses in the fund. You're going to use this account for emergencies, not for the motorcycle you've had your eye on that's suddenly for sale! If you do need to use this account for an emergency, your priority should be to work on replenishing the fund for the next unforeseen circumstance.

Prioritizing Debt Repayment

Yes, it's one of our least favorite aspects of life, but building a strong financial foundation includes paying off your debts. These may include credit cards, car and student loans, and your mortgage. Simply put, reducing debt before retirement results in less financial stress. In retirement, your income will likely be fixed or reduced compared to your previous salary. Having debt limits your ability to enjoy your retirement.

If leaving a financial legacy for your heirs is important to you, being debt-free allows you to pass on assets without the burden of handing down outstanding debts as well. It's essential to assess your unique financial situation, create a plan, and possibly consult with a financial advisor to make informed decisions that align with your retirement goals.

Last-Minute Strategies for Savings-Strapped Planners

If you find yourself in a situation where you're close to a financial goal—like retirement—and you feel like your savings are minimal, there are still some last-minute strategies you can consider. While it's always better to plan ahead, **these strategies can help you boost your savings in the final stretch:**

- Review your budget and cut any unnecessary expenses, such as dinners out, DoorDash food deliveries, or daily lattes. Do you want Starbucks every morning or a comfortable retirement? Be smart and divert any extra money to savings.

- Explore part-time jobs or side hustles, and sell unwanted belongings to generate extra income.

- Consider delaying your retirement a few years to continue earning and reducing the number of years you'll need to rely on your savings.

- Maximize contributions through your employer-sponsored retirement plan. Take advantage of any employer-matching and catch-up contributions.

- Refinance your debt in favor of a lower interest rate or payments to free up more money for savings.

- Consider moving assets in your portfolio to higher-performing investments (just be aware that these carry more risk).

- Check out government assistance programs or tax credits that might be available to you based on your income and financial situation.

Maximizing Your Contributions in the 11th Hour

Similar to the above scenario, if you find yourself close to the career finish line and want to maximize your contributions before retirement, there are some steps you can take to make the most of your remaining time. **The following are strategies for maximizing contributions as the clock starts ticking faster toward retirement:**

- If you're 50 or older, retirement plans allow you to pay larger amounts into them, which are called catch-up contributions.

- Open a second retirement account, such as a Roth IRA. If your spouse doesn't have a retirement account, you can open one and contribute on their behalf.

- Ensure that you don't miss any contributions by automating transfers or payments.

- Contribute to a Health Savings Account (HSA), which can be used for medical expenses in retirement.

- Maximize tax savings by contributing to your children's or grandchildren's 529 college-savings plans.

- Delay non-essential expenses and stick that money in savings.

- Speaking of savings, look for higher-yield savings accounts, like Ally Bank.

- Stick bonuses, tax refunds, or other unexpected windfalls into your retirement plans.

- If you're self-employed, contribute to a Simplified Employee Pension (SEP) or a Solo 401(k).

Exploring Side Hustle Income Streams

Side hustles are a great way to boost your finances, especially when you're looking to achieve specific financial goals or increase your savings. While you could get a second job delivering pizzas or working at the local store in the evenings and weekends, side hustles generally leverage your skills by offering services to others.

Did you always have a passion for writing or being creative? A side hustle centered around writing or graphic design could suit you, or perhaps creating and selling crafts and handmade goods on an online platform like Etsy.

Have a message you want to spread or just enjoy being on camera? You can consider making short-form videos on Instagram reels and TikTok, and as you build a following, you can promote products as an affiliate.

Or hey—maybe you've just got a passion for cooking and want to show the world. That's what Mary from her *Mary's Nest* YouTube channel decided to do a few years ago.

Recently retired, she wanted to turn her cooking skills into a side hustle. She enjoyed cooking with traditional foods and wanted to show the world how to do it, too. She hired a mentor for YouTube, learned the ropes, got her channel started, and within four years she's turned her YouTube channel into a thriving business with over one million subscribers.

You can see her channel here:

https://www.youtube.com/@MarysNest/videos

It truly is *never* too late to get started.

Below are a few more side hustle ideas to ponder:

- Love to share knowledge? Online tutoring, in which you can teach a language or something else related to an expertise. For example, you can join a platform like iTalki, where you can charge an hourly fee for one-on-one language lessons (in English, Spanish, or any other language you might be fluent in).

- Virtual assistance services such as email management, scheduling, data entry, and social media management are a great option if your organizational skills are top notch.

- Company's coming—you can rent out a spare room, vacation home, or even a parking space on platforms such as Airbnb.

- Write and self-publish ebooks on Amazon Kindle if you're great with the written word.

- If you've got a photographic eye, sell your snaps on Shutterstock or Adobe Stock.

- If fitness has always been your thing—or becomes your thing—you can become a personal trainer or yoga instructor.

- Gift of gab? Answer customer service calls for a company from your home office.

Choose a side hustle that aligns with your strengths and can fit into your schedule without causing burnout. Additionally, consider any legal or tax implications associated with your chosen gig. It's essential to have a clear understanding of how your extra income may impact your overall financial situation.

Downsizing (But Not Ditching) Your Dreams

This is a concept that emphasizes making practical adjustments to your goals without completely abandoning them. Life often involves unexpected changes or challenges, and it's important to adapt while still working toward your aspirations.

You may need to simplify your lifestyle or reassess your priorities, in which case you can adjust your financial goals to better match your current income, expenses, and overall financial situation. Emphasize personal growth and development over material things.

Remember that downsizing your dreams is *not* a sign of failure—it's a strategic and adaptive approach to align your aspirations with the reality of your current situation. By making thoughtful adjustments, you can continue progressing toward meaningful and attainable goals while embracing the ever-changing journey of life.

Building Savings, Building Dreams

This section encapsulates the idea that financial well-being and achieving one's dreams often go hand in hand. Many people like to live for the current moment and therefore find it burdensome to actively save for retirement. For them, automatic deductions from a paycheck are often easier.

The Rule of 25: Your Magic Number to Freedom

This is a simplified guideline used in financial planning to estimate the amount of savings needed for retirement. It's a rule of thumb derived from the concept of the 4% rule. The rule of 25 states that you can determine the amount you need to save for retirement by multiplying your desired annual retirement income by 25.

Here's the formula: Retirement Savings Goal = Annual Retirement Income × 25

For example, if you estimate that you'll need $40,000 per year in retirement income, your retirement savings goal would be $40,000 x 25 = $1,000,000.

This rule is based on the 4% rule, which suggests that if you can safely withdraw 4% of your retirement savings annually, you should have enough to last throughout a 30-year retirement. The rule of 25 provides a quick way to estimate the total savings needed to generate a specific income during retirement.

It's important to note that the rule of 25 is a general guideline and may not be accurate for everyone. Individual circumstances such as lifestyle, health, and inflation can significantly impact your retirement needs.

Automatic Contributions: Set It & Forget It

Here, we're referring to the practice of automating financial tasks, particularly in the context of automatic contributions. This strategy involves setting up recurring contributions or transfers to savings or investment accounts, allowing the process to occur automatically without the need for manual intervention.

Here's why setting it and forgetting it can be a beneficial financial approach:

- Automatic contributions ensure a consistent and regular savings or investment strategy. By automating the process, you're less likely to miss contributions, leading to more disciplined financial behavior.

- Establishing a routine of automated contributions reinforces financial discipline. It becomes a habit, making it easier to stick to your savings or investment goals over the long term.

- Automation minimizes the likelihood of procrastination. When contributions are automated, you don't have to remember or find the time to manually transfer funds, which reduces the chances of delaying or skipping contributions.

- Regular, automated contributions facilitate dollar-cost averaging, a strategy in which you invest a fixed amount at regular intervals, regardless of market fluctuations. This can result in a more balanced and potentially lower-risk investment approach over time.

- Setting up automatic contributions saves time. Once the initial setup is done, you don't have to spend time manually managing and transferring funds regularly.

- Automatic contributions can be aligned with specific financial goals, such as saving for a down payment, building an emergency fund, or contributing to retirement accounts. This targeted approach helps you stay on track toward achieving your objectives.

- Automation reduces the impact of emotional decision making on financial choices. When contributions are automatic, you're less likely to be influenced by market fluctuations or short-term financial news.

- Knowing that contributions are automated allows for better financial planning. You can budget more effectively knowing that a portion of your income is consistently directed toward savings or investments.

- If you have employer-sponsored retirement plans with matching contributions, automatic payments ensure that you're able to take full advantage of these benefits. Missing contributions could mean missing out on valuable employer matches.

- Essentially, automation provides peace of mind. You can be confident that you're consistently working toward your financial goals without having to actively manage every financial transaction.

To implement the "set it and forget it" strategy, contact your bank or financial institution to set up automatic transfers or contributions. You can specify the frequency (monthly, bi-weekly, etc.) and the amount to be transferred to your savings or investment accounts. Regularly review your contributions to ensure that they align with your financial goals, making adjustments as needed over time.

Catch-Up Contributions for Those Over 50

These are additional contributions that individuals aged 50 and older can make to certain retirement accounts to help them boost their savings as they approach retirement. These contributions are designed to assist older individuals in closing the gap between their current retirement savings and the amount needed for a financially secure retirement. **Below are some key points about these contributions:**

- **Eligible Retirement Accounts:** Catch-up contributions are typically allowed in certain tax-advantaged retirement accounts, such as 401(k)s,

403(b)s, IRAs (traditional and Roth), and the Thrift Savings Plan (TSP) for federal employees.

- **Annual Limits:** The regular annual contribution limits for retirement accounts are set by the Internal Revenue Service (IRS)[4]. As of 2024, **the catch-up contribution limits for individuals aged 50 and older are as follows:**

  - **401(k) and 403(b):** $7,500 in addition to the regular contribution limit.

  - **IRA (Traditional and Roth):** $1,000 in addition to the regular contribution limit.

  - **401(k) and 403(b) Catch-Up Contributions:** If you're 50 or older, you can contribute an extra $7,500 to your 401(k) or 403(b) in addition to the standard annual limit, which is $23,000 for 2024. This brings the total annual limit to $30,500.

  - **IRA Catch-Up Contributions:** For IRAs, the catch-up contribution limit for individuals aged 50 and older is an additional $1,000 on top of the standard annual limit, which is $7,000 for 2024. This makes the total annual limit $8,000.

In addition, catch-up contributions provide an opportunity for individuals to maximize their tax-advantaged retirement savings. Contributions to Traditional 401(k)s and IRAs are tax-deductible, while contributions to Roth 401(k)s and Roth IRAs are made with after-tax dollars but offer tax-free withdrawals in retirement.

Also, some employers may match a percentage of employee contributions to retirement accounts. Catch-up contributions could potentially increase the amount of matching contributions you receive from your employer.

Catch-up contributions are particularly beneficial for individuals who may have started saving for retirement later in their careers or experienced periods with lower savings. These additional contributions can help accelerate savings growth.

While there are no income limits for making traditional IRA contributions, there *are* income limits for making Roth IRA contributions. Make sure to check the IRS guidelines to ensure that you meet the eligibility criteria for the type of IRA you want to contribute to.

It's important to note that contribution limits and rules may and do change, so it's advisable to check with the IRS or a financial advisor for the most up-to-date information. Additionally, consider consulting with a financial professional to determine the best strategy for your specific financial situation and retirement goals.

Staying the Course with Periodic Reviews & Adjustments

Remaining committed to your financial path involves the ongoing practice of regularly reviewing and finetuning your financial plan. **Consider these key elements to stay on track with your financial goals through regular assessments and necessary adjustments:**

- Schedule regular reviews of your financial situation. This could be done quarterly, semi-annually, or annually depending on your preferences and any significant life changes.

- Assess your budget periodically to ensure that it aligns with your current income, expenses, and savings goals. Adjust spending categories as needed and look for areas to optimize. For example, maybe you can shrink your travel budget by deciding to keep this year's travels domestic instead of abroad (it's not nearly as exotic as Cancun, but you'll thank yourself later).

- Review your investment portfolio regularly to ensure that it aligns with your risk tolerance, time horizon, and financial goals. As you get older, it's typically better to shift more of your assets to less volatile investments. For example, while your portfolio may have been more heavily invested in the S&P 500 in your 20s, 30s, and 40s, it may be wise to shift a little more over to bonds and treasuries as you get into your 50s and beyond.

- Consult with an advisor for professional insights.

Choosing Your Weapons: What Are the Best Accounts for You?

Selecting the most suitable financial accounts is a critical aspect of managing your money effectively. While placing money in a checking, savings, or money-market account is safe, the interest rates are very small. A certificate of deposit provides slightly higher interest rates and is great for a longer-term saving goal. For retirement savings, you'll want to choose one of the established types of accounts.

Understanding Different Retirement Account Options

The choice of retirement accounts is often influenced by your work situation, employment status, and the retirement benefits provided by your employer. If you work for a corporation, you'll have different options than if you're self-employed.

Traditional IRA vs. Roth IRA

As mentioned above, a traditional IRA (Individual Retirement Account) is a tax-advantaged retirement savings account in which contributions may be tax-deductible. The investments in the account grow tax-deferred, and withdrawals during retirement are subject to income tax. Traditional IRAs have Required Minimum Distributions (RMDs) starting at age 72, and contributions aren't limited by income. Early withdrawals before age 59½ may incur penalties, and the account provides a tax-efficient way to save for retirement—especially if you expect to be in a lower tax bracket in retirement.

Conversely, a Roth IRA is a retirement savings account in which contributions are made with after-tax dollars, allowing for tax-free withdrawals in retirement. It has no Required Minimum Distributions, income limits for contributions, and provides flexibility for early withdrawals of contributions without penalties. A Roth IRA is advantageous for those expecting a similar or higher tax bracket in retirement, and it can be a tax-efficient way to save for the future.

Choose a traditional IRA if you want immediate tax deductions, are in a higher tax bracket now but expect a lower one in retirement, and are comfortable with Required Minimum Distributions (RMDs). On the other hand, opt for a Roth IRA if you prioritize tax-free withdrawals in retirement, expect to be in a similar or higher tax bracket, value flexibility in withdrawals, and want to avoid RMDs. Consider your income, risk tolerance, and withdrawal needs, and consult with a financial advisor to make an informed decision based on your unique financial situation and goals.

Employer-Sponsored Retirement Plans

Employer-sponsored retirement plans are exactly what they sound like—retirement savings programs offered by employers to help their employees save for their retirement. These plans typically come with tax advantages and often include employer contributions.

401(k): Employees can contribute a portion of their pre-tax salary to this plan, and employers often offer matching contributions. The contributions and investment gains within the plan grow tax-deferred until withdrawal. Some plans also provide a Roth 401(k) option with after-tax contributions and tax-free withdrawals in retirement. Key features include automatic payroll deductions, employer matching, tax advantages, portability, vesting schedules, potential loan options, and required minimum distributions starting at age 72. Early withdrawals before age 59½ may incur penalties.

403(b): This is designed for employees of non-profit organizations, schools, and certain tax-exempt entities. Similar to a 401(k), it allows employees to contribute a portion of their pre-tax salary to the plan, with potential matching contributions from the employer. Contributions and investment gains grow tax-deferred until withdrawal. The plan offers automatic payroll deductions, potential employer matching, tax advantages, portability, and early withdrawal penalties before age 59½. Participants may have the option to take loans from the plan, and required minimum distributions (RMDs) generally start at age 72.

457(b): Primarily available for employees of state and local governments and certain tax-exempt organizations, this allows employees to defer a portion of their salary into the plan on a pre-tax basis. Contributions and investment gains grow tax-deferred until withdrawal. The plan offers features such as automatic payroll deductions, tax advantages, and potential early withdrawal penalties before age 59½. Unlike some other retirement plans, 457(b)s don't typically have a 10% early withdrawal penalty, making them more flexible. Participants may also have the option to take loans from the plan, and required minimum distributions (RMDs) generally start at age 72.

Small Business & Self-Employed Retirement Plans

The following are the basic plans for those that are self-employed or own a small business:

A **Solo 401(k)** is a retirement plan for self-employed individuals or small business owners with no employees. It allows both personal and employer contributions, providing flexibility in savings. Contributions are tax-deductible, and the plan offers higher contribution limits. It's relatively easy to set up and has a Roth option for tax-free withdrawals in retirement. Solo 401(k)s don't require mandatory withdrawals during the account owner's lifetime. They're a flexible and tax-efficient way for self-employed individuals to save for retirement.

A **SEP-IRA (Simplified Employee Pension)** is a retirement plan for self-employed people and small businesses. Only the employer can contribute, those contributions are tax-deductible, and the amount contributed can vary each year. Setting up and managing a SEP-IRA is simple, with fewer administrative tasks. While there's no Roth option, it provides a tax advantage by reducing taxable income. There's flexibility in deciding whether to contribute each year, and it's also accessible for employees.

A **SIMPLE IRA (Savings Incentive Match Plan for Employees)** is a retirement plan for small businesses with up to 100 employees. Both employers and employees can contribute, and it has lower administrative costs than some other plans. Contributions are tax-deductible for the employer, and employees' contributions are made before taxes. While there's no Roth option with this one either, it's easy to set up and employers have flexibility in making contributions. Early withdrawals may have penalties, but it's a straightforward plan to encourage retirement savings in smaller workplaces.

A **Defined Benefit Plan** is a retirement savings method in which employers promise a specific benefit to employees upon retirement. It's suitable for businesses with stable income. Employers, not employees, contribute to the plan, with the amount determined by an actuarial calculation. This plan offers a predictable retirement income for employees and comes with tax advantages for employers. While it provides a guaranteed benefit, it's more complex to set up and typically requires professional assistance.

Key Takeaways

- The type of retirement plan available depends on your employment status.

- There are several ways to determine how much you'll need in retirement, including the 4% rule and the rule of 25.

- When budgeting for retirement, be sure to factor in inflation and cost of living increases.

- If you find yourself short on funds and nearing retirement, there are several courses of action, including catch-up contributions or delaying retirement for the time being.

- Saving for retirement may mean delaying immediate gratification, but the payoff in the long run is worth it.

Chapter 3

Retirement Investment Planning for Smart People

"It's not how much money you make, but how much money you keep, how hard it works for you, and how many generations you keep it for."

-Robert Kiyosaki, author of Rich Dad, Poor Dad

Creating an effective retirement plan is easily achievable with a few simple steps, two of which include understanding your finances and learning about investments. To accomplish this, you can use online tools, explore accounts with tax advantages, and seek the advice of a financial planner.

Deciding If You Need a Financial Planner

When making this important decision, look at your goals for the future, your knowledge of financial matters, and the complexity of your financial situation. **Below are some scenarios in which a financial planner could be the right choice for you:**

- If your financial situation is more complex, involving multiple sources of income, investments, or significant assets.

- If you have specific goals such as purchasing a home, financing your child's education, or retirement planning, a financial planner can help you create a roadmap to achieve those objectives.

- If you're unsure about investment strategies, risk tolerance, and portfolio management.

- If you find that you don't have or don't want to spend the time learning how to handle financial matters.

- If you face significant life events such as marriage, divorce, the birth of a child, a job change—and, yes, retirement—that can impact your financial situation.

- If your tax situation is complex.

- If you prefer having a professional to guide you through financial decisions, provide personalized advice, and offer peace of mind.

Financial planners consider *all* aspects of your financial life. Opting for a holistic approach to your finances allows a financial planner to formulate a comprehensive plan specifically tailored to your individual circumstances.

What Financial Planners Do & Who Can Benefit

Financial planners provide advice on various aspects of financial planning including budgeting, saving, investing, retirement planning, tax planning, and estate planning. Their primary goal is to create a comprehensive financial strategy that's specific to your needs and goals.

Below are some key activities that financial planners typically engage in:

- Analyze their clients' current financial situation including income, expenses, assets, and liabilities.

- Work with clients to establish short-term and long-term financial goals such as purchasing a residence, saving for your child's education, or retirement planning.

- Help clients create and stick to a budget, as well as develop strategies for saving and building an emergency fund.

- Provide guidance on investment options based on the client's risk tolerance, timeline, and financial objectives. These may include recommending stocks, bonds, mutual funds, and other investment vehicles.

- Help clients plan for retirement by estimating how much they need to save, recommending retirement accounts, and developing strategies to generate income during retirement.

- Aid clients in reducing tax obligations by engaging in strategic planning, leveraging tax deductions, and optimizing investment portfolios to minimize tax liability.

- Assess the insurance requirements of clients and suggest suitable coverage options.

- Help clients create an estate plan, which may involve drafting wills, establishing trusts, and minimizing estate taxes.

As an example, let's take Jack and Mary, a married couple in their early 50s. Their oldest daughter Penny just graduated high school and is headed to college in the fall. They've been putting some money away for her education for the past several years but fear that they'll fall short.

The couple both worked steadily and put money in their 401(k) plans at work, but they're considering reducing their contributions while Penny is in college.

However, they aren't sure how this will affect them later. Jack's colleague recommends a financial planner to help them crunch the numbers, and they have an initial consultation next week.

The Financial Planner Litmus Test: A Self-Assessment Quiz

To determine whether you need a financial planner, you can ask yourself a series of questions to assess your financial situation and goals. This questionnaire can help you gauge whether hiring a financial planner might be beneficial for you.

- Do you have clearly defined financial goals for the short and long term?

- Is your financial situation becoming more complex?

- Do you possess both the time and expertise required to effectively manage your investments?

- Have you experienced or anticipated significant life changes (e.g., marriage, divorce, retirement, inheritance)?

- Do you feel confident in your ability to create a budget and stick to it?

- Is your tax situation complex?

- Do you lack knowledge about insurance options and coverage?

- Would you benefit from a holistic approach to your finances, including estate planning?

- Do you prefer having a professional to consult for financial advice and peace of mind?

- Are you approaching retirement or already retired?

Remember—these questions are meant as a guide, and there's no right or wrong answer. If you find that several of these questions resonate with your situation, it may be worth considering a consultation with a financial planner to explore how their services align with your needs and goals.

Tips for Picking Your Perfect Money Guru

Choosing the appropriate financial planner or financial expert for your requirements is a pivotal decision that can have a substantial impact on your financial well-being. **Let's look at some tips to help you pick the perfect planner for your situation:**

- Look for credentials such as certified financial planner (CFP), chartered financial analyst (CFA), or other relevant certifications. Check their education, professional memberships, and any additional qualifications that demonstrate expertise in financial planning.[5]

- Seek out an individual who has experience working with clients in situations similar to yours.

- Choose someone whose expertise aligns with your specific situation.

- Opt for a planner who operates as a fiduciary (someone who prioritizes your financial well-being over their own interests).

- Understand the fee structure before committing. Financial planners may charge a flat fee, percentage of assets, or an hourly rate. Ensure that the fee arrangement is transparent and that there are no hidden costs.

- Make certain that you're comfortable with the planner's communication style. Choose someone with whom you feel at ease sharing personal financial information.

- Consider the technology and tools that the planner uses. In our digital age, many financial planners leverage technology for virtual meetings, financial planning software, and online document sharing. Make sure that their methods align with your values.

- Ensure that the financial expert is registered with the relevant regulatory bodies. In the United States, for instance, this may involve verifying registration with the Securities and Exchange Commission (SEC) or state regulatory authorities.

Keep in mind that selecting the right financial expert is a personal choice, so take the necessary time to extensively research and interview potential candidates before reaching a decision. Many financial planners provide an initial consultation just for this purpose.

Creating a Retirement Income Plan

A smart retirement plan combines stocks, bonds, mutual funds, annuities, and real estate for a balanced approach to growth and stability.

Getting Literate with Stocks, Bonds & Mutual Funds

Understanding these building blocks for financial literacy is essential to understanding your retirement portfolio, as most formal accounts consist of these items. **Let's break them down:**

- Stocks represent ownership in a company, and their worth may vary depending on the company's performance and market conditions.

- Bonds are financial instruments that involve investors lending funds to an entity, like a government or corporation. In return, investors receive regular interest payments and the repayment of the principal amount upon maturity.

- Mutual funds pool funds from numerous investors and invest them in a diversified portfolio composed of stocks, bonds, or other securities.

Understanding the basics of these investment options, including their risks and returns, is crucial for making informed decisions and building a well-balanced investment portfolio.

The Role of Real Estate & REITs in Your Retirement Portfolio

Incorporating real estate into your retirement portfolio can help diversify and strengthen it. Real estate investments can provide both income and potential appreciation when included in your portfolio. One way to invest in real estate is through direct ownership of properties—rental income can supplement your retirement income and give you some extra monthly cash flow, and property values may appreciate over time.

Plus, it can be done somewhat passively if you have the right systems in place, like a reliable property manager who can find and vet out tenants, as well as a good local realtor who can send you properties in your price range. Just be aware that even when it's passive, it can still have its headaches—you should plan for periods of potential vacancies, missed payments from tenants, or even needing to evict a problem tenant from time to time.

If you want exposure to real estate without any of those potential headaches of owning your own properties, real estate investment trusts (REITs) offer another avenue, allowing you to invest in a variety of properties without purchasing them directly. REITs often pay dividends, providing a potential income stream for retirees.

Here's how REITs work: They pool funds from numerous investors to purchase, manage, and operate income-producing real estate, which can include a variety of properties like apartment complexes, office buildings, hotels, or shopping centers.

Two primary types of REITs exist. Equity REITs predominantly own and manage income-producing real estate properties, deriving income from rent collection and property appreciation. Mortgage REITs (mREITs) invest in mortgages or mortgage-backed securities, generating income from the interest on these loans.

Investors can acquire shares of publicly traded REITs on stock exchanges, offering a liquid and accessible avenue for real estate investment. REITs are legally obligated to distribute a substantial portion of their income to shareholders, making them appealing to investors seeking regular income. However, they also expose investors to the risks associated with the real estate market and its fluctuations.

There are some other notable downsides to investing in REITs instead of buying your own properties. You can usually expect lower returns and a lack of control, as you aren't the one managing the fund yourself. Also, you won't get the tax advantages of actually *owning* real estate—depreciation deductions, mortgage and interest deductions, and property tax deductions won't apply to you.

Understanding the Bucket Strategy

This is a retirement income planning approach that involves dividing your investment portfolio into different "buckets" based on time to retirement and risk tolerance. The strategy is designed to provide a systematic and organized way to manage withdrawals in retirement while ensuring a mix of safety and growth. **Here's a simplified breakdown:**

- The **immediate bucket** contains cash and short-term investments, covering one to two years' worth of living expenses. It provides a stable source of income, ensuring that you have readily available funds without having to sell investments in a market downturn.

- The **intermediate bucket** holds assets that are slightly more aggressive than the immediate bucket, and they may include bonds and conservative investments. The goal is to generate moderate returns while still maintaining a level of stability. This bucket typically covers expenses for the next three to ten years.

- The **long-term bucket** is the most growth oriented. It encompasses investments like stocks and other assets that have the potential for increased returns over an extended timeframe. This bucket is designed to fund expenses beyond the ten-year mark and allows for a more aggressive investment approach.

Ultimately, the bucket strategy is a method for retirees to handle market fluctuations. In good times, they use money from safer buckets and let the riskier one grow. During tough times, they temporarily use safer buckets to avoid selling risky assets at a low. It's vital to adjust the buckets as you get older or as the market changes. This strategy aims to balance between keeping your money safe and letting it grow, and provides a structured plan for retirees to manage their income throughout retirement.

Are Annuities Your Friends or Your Foes?

An annuity is a financial instrument that delivers a sequence of regular payments for a defined duration or throughout your lifetime. To purchase an annuity, you have the option to either provide a single lump sum payment or make multiple payments to the annuity provider. In return, the provider guarantees a stream of income, which can start immediately or at a later date.

There are different types of annuities. Fixed annuities guarantee a predetermined payout, variable annuities fluctuate based on the performance of underlying investments, and indexed annuities are tied to the performance of a market index. Annuities can provide a reliable income source and are often used to address the risk of outliving one's savings in retirement.

Are annuities good or bad for you? Well, it depends on your needs. Annuities can be helpful if you want a steady income in retirement and don't mind some limitations on accessing your money. They provide stability and protection from market ups and downs. However, they can be complicated, with fees and restrictions on getting your money. If you value flexibility and lower costs, other options might be better. Before deciding, carefully consider your goals and talk to a financial advisor to understand if annuities are a good fit for you.

The Top 3 Strategies for Investment Success

Retirement planning involves key strategies like diversification, rebalancing, and understanding risk tolerance. Together, these principles offer a straightforward guide for creating a resilient retirement plan based on your unique financial situation.

Diversification: Don't Put All Your Eggs in One Basket

Playing a crucial role in retirement planning, diversification serves as a strategy to help protect your savings and investments. In retirement planning, it means spreading your money across different types of investments like stocks, bonds, mutual funds, and real estate. The objective is to establish a well-balanced portfolio that doesn't rely too heavily on any single type of investment.

Diversification lessens the impact of a single investment on your portfolio. Investments have different levels of risk, and they may react to changes in the market. While risk isn't eliminated through diversification, it can help make your retirement portfolio less volatile.

Rebalancing: Keeping Your Portfolio in Check

Rebalancing means adjusting your investment mix periodically to keep the risk and return at the levels you want. As time progresses, the values of various assets in your portfolio can shift. Rebalancing entails the buying or selling of assets to realign with your initial investment plan.

The goal here is to make sure your portfolio's risk matches your comfort level and financial goals. For example, if stocks perform well and become a larger part of your portfolio than you intended, rebalancing might mean selling stocks and buying other assets like bonds or cash to restore the original mix.

Rebalancing helps control risk by avoiding the portfolio becoming too focused on high-performing (and potentially more volatile) assets. Regularly reviewing and finetuning your retirement portfolio—whether on an annual or semi-annual basis—guarantees that your investment strategy remains in harmony with your risk tolerance and long-term objectives. This habit fosters a more stable and disciplined approach to retirement planning.

Risk Tolerance: Walking the Fine Line

In retirement planning, risk tolerance refers to how comfortable you are with the possibility of your investments changing in value. The goal is to position your investment strategy with your comfort level, financial goals, and the time until your retirement. If you can handle more ups and downs, you might choose riskier investments for potentially higher returns such as cryptocurrency investments. However, if you prefer stability, you may opt for safer investments like bonds or treasuries. As you near retirement, you might want to adjust your investments toward a more conservative approach, which will ensure a safer account balance. Regularly check your risk tolerance, especially during major life changes, to make sure that your investment strategy matches your comfort and long-term goals.

Today's Alternative Investments: Risks vs. Potentials

Alternative investments for retirement accounts introduce diverse options beyond traditional stocks and bonds, aiming to enhance portfolio diversification and potentially improve returns. These options include assets like real estate, commodities, cryptocurrencies, and private equity funds.

While they can offer unique opportunities, it's crucial to recognize that alternative investments often come with higher risk and complexity. Investors considering alternatives for retirement should carefully assess their risk tolerance, understand the specific characteristics of each investment, and, if needed, seek advice from financial professionals. The goal is to strike a balance that aligns with long-term retirement objectives while acknowledging the potential benefits and risks associated with alternative investments.

Exploring Cryptocurrency, Commodities & ETFs

These three relatively recent appearances on the financial scene may be cause for some head scratching, so let's examine each of them closely below.

Commodities

These are raw materials or agricultural products traded on exchanges. They're divided into two main types: hard commodities (like metals and energy resources, usually mined) and soft commodities (such as agricultural products, grown instead of mined).

Commodities are traded on exchanges, and their prices are influenced by factors like supply and demand, geopolitical events, weather, and global economics. Investors can gain exposure to commodities through various means such as commodity futures contracts, commodity-focused mutual funds, or exchange-traded funds (ETFs) that track commodity indexes.

Below are some of the most common commodities:

- **Gold:** This is often considered a safe-haven asset and a hedge against inflation and economic uncertainty. Investors often turn to gold during periods of high market volatility.

- **Silver:** This is also considered a store of value, but its price tends to be a bit more volatile than gold.

- **Precious Metals ETFs:** As mentioned, ETFs like these track the performance of precious metals like gold, silver, and platinum.

ETFs

ETFs are like baskets of investments (such as stocks or bonds) that you can buy or sell on the stock exchange. They provide instant diversification, meaning that you invest in various assets at once. ETFs are traded like individual stocks throughout the day, making them flexible and easy to buy or sell. They're cost-effective, transparent, and a popular choice for both short-term and long-term investors.

Some of the most common ETFs are those that track the S&P 500, like SPDR S&P 500 ETF (SPY) and Vanguard S&P 500 ETF (VOO). Other popular ones include SPDR Gold Shares (GLD), which tracks the price of gold, and iShares MSCI Emerging Markets ETF (EEM), which provides exposure to emerging market equities.

ETFs in general can give you more broad market exposure, but make sure to do your own research before choosing one to invest in.

Cryptocurrency

Unless you've been living in a cave, you've definitely heard of Bitcoin by this point. But you might not know exactly what it is, other than that it's had some high highs, some low lows, and can be volatile.

Maybe it's piqued your interest but felt too risky or complicated to get into it. So let's examine it—and cryptocurrencies as a whole—even further, and whether or not they could have a place in your retirement portfolio.

To start, cryptocurrencies are digital currencies that use secure technology called blockchain. In contrast to conventional currency, these are decentralized, indicating that they operate without government or central authority oversight. All transactions are documented on a public ledger, guaranteeing both transparency and security. Cryptocurrencies use cryptography to protect transactions and have a limited supply. Bitcoin was the first kind of cryptocurrency out there, but now there are thousands of others, such as Ethereum and Litecoin, both known as "altcoins." People use cryptocurrencies for online transactions and investments, but they're also known for their price fluctuations and regulatory issues.

Over the years, the crypto market has tended to go in big cycles. Bitcoin has flashed as high as $20k, crashed back down below $5k during COVID, and shot all the way back up to over $60k multiple times. You can see why it's known for its volatility. But should *you* dabble in a little crypto?

Well, it can be a good idea to have a little cryptocurrency exposure, even if it's just 1% to 2% of your portfolio. That way, it's not the end of the world if it crashes, but if it hits another volatile upswing, that 1% to 2% might quickly turn into 5% to 10%, which can bolster your retirement funds nicely (although you may want to rebalance things at that point).And the good thing is that it's now easier than ever to invest in crypto, as there's a Bitcoin ETF and a forthcoming Ethereum ETF.

A Bitcoin ETF is like a stock that you can buy on a regular stock exchange. You own shares in the ETF as opposed to actual Bitcoin—the price is based on Bitcoin's value. It's a more straightforward way for investors to get involved with Bitcoin without directly dealing with the cryptocurrency.That said, if you want to own your own Bitcoin, you can buy it on an exchange like CoinBase. From there, if you'd like to self-custody your Bitcoin, you can transfer it to a hardware wallet (like a Trezor). Just make sure that you safely secure your backup keys and passwords.

Now keep in mind that controversy still exists regarding the viability of cryptocurrencies, with many discussions revolving around their potential as substantial opportunities or mere speculative bubbles. Bitcoin and Ethereum, among other cryptocurrencies, have demonstrated noteworthy expansion, capturing interest as assets distinguished by distinctive features. On one hand, proponents argue that cryptocurrencies represent the future of finance, offering decentralized systems and a hedge against traditional market volatility. On the other, skeptics view them as speculative and highly volatile assets, comparing them to historical financial bubbles.

If you're contemplating investments in cryptocurrencies, assess your risk tolerance, engage in research, and remain updated on market changes. And if you *do* start buying, you can download an app like Delta that allows you to input your crypto purchases and easily track your portfolio.

P2P Lending & Crowdfunding: Bank-Free Newcomers

In the world of retirement planning, it's essential to consider alternative investments, and two standout options are P2P lending (peer-to-peer lending) and crowdfunding. This section explores how these alternatives, both free from traditional banking, can diversify retirement portfolios and potentially offer unique benefits.

P2P lending involves individuals borrowing and lending money directly through online platforms. Instead of going through a bank, you can connect on these platforms, with some users looking for loans and others willing to lend money. This process happens online, covering various borrowing needs like personal, business, or educational loans. Borrowers get loans from a group of individual lenders, and interest rates are often competitive. Nevertheless, there are obviously some inherent risks, including the potential for borrowers to default on their loans.

If you're interested in P2P lending, you can look into some of the most popular P2P platforms like LendingClub (which facilitates loans for personal and small business purchases), Prosper (which offers personal loans and investment opportunities to investors), and Funding Circle (which focuses on small business loans).

On the other end of the spectrum, Crowdfunding in the context of retirement planning means using online platforms to gather small amounts of money from many people for a specific project or business. Some people explore crowdfunding to create additional income sources during retirement. For instance, they might start a small business or pursue a project that could generate some extra cash. Nonetheless, exercising caution is crucial, as success isn't assured and there are associated risks. Careful research and consideration are necessary before using crowdfunding as part of retirement planning.

You may have heard of popular crowdfunding platforms like Kickstarter (which allows you to raise funds for creative products, projects, and ideas) and SeedInvest (which allows accredited investors to invest in early-stage startups). Other crowdfunding platforms worth looking into include Indiegogo, GoFundMe, and CrowdCube. But always remember to consider your options carefully before committing to this avenue.

Avoiding Common Investing Blunders & Temptations

You'd be forgiven for making any of the below mishaps, as retirement planning is a first for all of us at some point and errors are bound to occur. But let's examine some frequent follies below so that, hopefully, none of them happen to you.

Beware the Perils of Chasing Returns

Retirement planning investors who engage in chasing returns might allocate their funds to investments that have experienced recent success, driven by the desire to capture quick and significant profits. However, this approach carries risks, as historical performance isn't always a good indication of future outcomes.

Chasing returns can lead to poor investment decisions, increased exposure to market volatility, and potential losses if the chosen assets or strategies don't sustain their previous performance. It contrasts with a more strategic and disciplined investment approach that considers long-term goals, risk tolerance, and a diversified portfolio.

Instead of chasing returns, it's better to adopt a diversified and disciplined approach. This involves setting realistic long-term goals, creating a well-balanced portfolio that aligns with those goals and their risk tolerance, and regularly reviewing and adjusting the portfolio as needed without reacting impulsively to short-term market movements.

To illustrate the danger of chasing returns, let's take a look at George's situation. He's in his early 60s and has decided to put 1% of his $1 million dollar investment portfolio into crypto. That $10,000 quickly multiplied by five to $50,000, as Bitcoin and the other altcoins he chose exploded upward. Instead of taking some profit and transferring a portion to lower risk investments like bonds and treasuries, he gets excited, decides to let it ride, and even puts another $20,000 into the crypto market.

As it turns out, this ends up being the very top of the cycle, and the crypto markets retrace 80% over the following six months. During that time, George tells himself that it's only temporary and that the market will return to its highs once again. But it doesn't come back for another three years, and many of the altcoins he invested in don't survive to the next cycle or make it back to their original highs

Instead of profiting $40,000 on his original investment, his $70k (the $10k that had multiplied by five and the other $20k he put in) is now worth just $14k. Had he started selling and repositioning things on the way up, he would've made a much larger profit and came out on top.

Frauds & Scams: Protecting Your Hard-Earned Money

By staying vigilant, conducting thorough research, and seeking advice from trusted sources, you can reduce the risk of falling victim to scams and frauds in retirement planning. You've heard the old advice: If something seems too good to be true, it likely is, and exercising caution is key to protecting your financial well-being. [6]

Let's look at some tips to avoid scams:

- Do your research before committing any funds to a new investment opportunity. Be skeptical of "get-rich-quick" schemes and high-return promises, as they often signal potential scams.

- Take your time to evaluate options and don't succumb to pressure or greed.

- Be cautious of communications from sources that come out of nowhere, especially if they're through cold calls, emails, or messages.

- Clearly understand the fees and costs associated with any financial product or service.

- Guard your personal and financial information closely. Establish trust before sharing personal details—be sure that any online transactions or communications are secure.

- If using online investment platforms, ensure that they're reputable and regulated.

- Seek advice from trusted sources such as certified financial planners, reputable financial institutions, or government agencies.

Report any suspicious activity to agencies such as the Federal Trade Commission (FTC) or your country's equivalent consumer protection agency. If you suspect that you've been the victim of a scam, take steps to protect your accounts.

The following are some additional ways you can protect yourself and improve security:

- **Use Strong Passwords:** Create strong, unique passwords for your online accounts and financial institutions. Use a combination of letters, numbers, and special characters, and avoid using easily guessable information such as birthdays or pet names.

- **Enable Two-Factor Authentication (2FA):** This adds an extra layer of security by requiring a second form of verification, generally through a text or an authentication app like Authy.

- **Update Your Software:** Keep your computer, smartphone, and other devices updated with the latest security patches and software updates. Use reputable antivirus and antimalware software to protect against viruses, malware, and other online threats.

Staying Wary of "Hot Stocks" That Can Flop

While the allure of quick and substantial returns is enticing, hot stocks often come with elevated risks. These stocks may experience inflated valuations driven by market speculation, media hype, or short-term trends. Investors must exercise caution and conduct extensive research before investing in these widely popular yet potentially volatile assets. Thorough due diligence should encompass an analysis of the company's fundamentals, market trends, and its potential long-term viability. Avoiding the temptation to chase after hot stocks without careful consideration can help you mitigate risks and maintain a more stable and sustainable investment strategy.

Portfolio Overconfidence: Retiring Prematurely

Being too confident in your investment portfolio and retiring too early can obviously be quite risky. If you overestimate the stability of your investments—especially in changing markets—you might exhaust your retirement savings and struggle to maintain your desired lifestyle. To avoid this, regularly review your retirement plans, considering market fluctuations and unforeseen expenses. Seek guidance from financial experts and stay realistic about your portfolio's performance to ensure a more secure and well-thought-out retirement.

No Surprises: Transparency on Investment Fees

Knowing all about the fees associated with your investments is important to avoid surprises and make smart financial decisions. This includes understanding management fees, transaction costs, and any other charges. Clear information on fees helps you know the real cost of your investments, compare different options, and plan your finances without any unexpected setbacks. Regularly reviewing and understanding the fees is a smart move for sound financial management.

Also, keep in mind that those fees can add up quickly. Let's say that you invested $100,000 30 years ago at a 1% annual investment fee. This may not seem like much, **but look how it adds up over time:**

Without the fee, if we assume a 7% annual growth rate, that $100,000 would grow to $761k over that 30-year span. Not bad!

But with that 1% fee, instead of growing at 7% annually, you'd only grow at 6%. That $761k would turn into just $574k after those 30 years, costing you over $186,000 in returns!

Thankfully, it's easy to avoid hefty investment fees like these. For example, ETFs and index funds tend to have lower fees compared to actively managed funds, and they often have the same or better returns.

Taking a Loan that Devalues Your 401(k)

When you borrow from your 401(k), you're essentially taking money out of your retirement account, which can reduce the overall value of your investments. Additionally, fees and taxes may be imposed if you fail to repay the loan according to the terms set by your plan.

This devaluation occurs because the borrowed amount is typically no longer invested in the market, potentially missing out on potential gains. Moreover, when you repay the loan, you may be doing so with after-tax dollars, and the interest paid goes back into your 401(k) but doesn't fully compensate for the missed market growth.

It's important to carefully consider the impact on your retirement savings before considering a loan from your retirement plan. Explore alternative options, and if you choose to proceed, ensure that you fully understand the terms, repayment schedule, and potential consequences to make an informed decision.

Succumbing to Fear or Greed

Driven by fear, investors might make impulsive decisions such as selling investments during market downturns, which could take years to recover losses. Acting out of greed may lead to taking excessive risks, like pursuing high returns without considering the risks.

Both fear and greed can disrupt a well-thought-out investment strategy and result in significant financial setbacks. It's crucial for investors to maintain a disciplined and rational approach, focusing on long-term goals, risk tolerance, and a diversified portfolio. Regularly reviewing and adjusting the investment strategy based on a well-defined plan, rather than reacting emotionally to short-term market fluctuations, can contribute to more successful and sustainable financial outcomes.

Key Takeaways

- The right financial planner can guide you through life changes and help design a roadmap to a prosperous retirement. Choose wisely.

- In addition to stocks, bonds, and mutual funds, retirement planners can explore real estate funds, commodities, cryptocurrency, and P2P lending, among other options.

- The top three strategies for investing are diversification, rebalancing, and risk tolerance.

- Investing is a long-term strategy. Avoid common pitfalls associated with trying to "beat-the-market" or "get-rich-quick" schemes.

- The bucket strategy will ensure that you have money for today's expenses and tomorrow's retirement.

Chapter 4

Minimizing the Tax Bite on Your Retirement Income

"The legal right of a taxpayer to decrease the amount of what otherwise would be his taxes, or altogether to avoid them, by means which the law permits, cannot be doubted."

-George Sutherland, former Supreme Court Justice (1922 to 1938)

One of the only certainties in life is that the government *is* going to tax your retirement income. If you set aside money in your 401(k) account, you were able to save on taxes—that is, until you retire, and then it's counted as income. If you invested in a Roth IRA, you used after-tax dollars. Either way, the government gets its money. And if you have an estate to pass on to your heirs, they face tax burdens as well.

But as Justice Sutherland reminds us above, it is your right to take advantage of any strategies that can lower that burden. In this chapter, we explore the different ways to keep more of your money—from donating to charities to converting to Roth IRAs and setting up charitable trusts.

Getting a Clear View of Your Retirement Tax Picture

Understanding your particular tax scenario is a key factor in keeping as much of your retirement income as possible. You need to look at your income sources and how each one of them is taxed. Also, it's paramount to consider credits and deductions.

How Different Types of Income Are Taxed

Different types of income are taxed in various ways, and taxation can depend on factors such as the source of income, its nature, and the applicable tax laws.

- **Earned income** is taxed at the federal and state level. Taxes for Social Security and Medicare are taken from your paycheck. If you're self-employed, you handle both the employer and employee parts of these taxes. Income tax is then applied to your net self-employment earnings.

- **Investment income** is generally taxed as ordinary income. Taxes on dividends are at capital gains rates, but it depends on the holding period and the type of dividend. Gains from the sale of investments are taxed based on whether they're short- or long-term gains. Short-term gains are taxed as ordinary income, while long-term gains have a lower tax rate.

- **Traditional IRA and 401(k) distributions** are taxed at regular income tax rates when withdrawn in retirement. Roth IRA distributions are tax-free, as they were funded with after-tax dollars. Social Security is taxed depending on how much income you have.

- **Rental income** is taxed at ordinary income tax rates. However, you should take advantage of available deductions like mortgage interest, property taxes, and depreciation.

- **Business income** is taxed based on the structure of the business. Partnerships and S corporations pass income to the owner's individual tax returns.

- **Unemployment compensation** is taxed as regular income.

- **Gifts and inheritance** recipients don't pay taxes on the amount received, but the estate may pay taxes.

- **Alimony** is considered taxable income for the receiver, but deductible for the payer. Child support isn't considered taxable income.

- **Gambling winnings, awards, and prizes** have different tax treatments. Check the latest IRS rules for specifics related to these windfalls.

The Impact of Taxes on Social Security Benefits

Tax on Social Security benefits depends on factors such as total income and filing status. Federal income taxes may apply to Social Security benefits if your combined income surpasses a specific threshold.

The IRS employs a formula that considers adjusted gross income, nontaxable interest, and half of your Social Security benefits to calculate combined income. Two distinct thresholds and corresponding taxable rates are applied.

If you're a single filer with a combined income of $25,000 to $34,000 (the joint filers' range is from $32,000 to $44,000), expect to have 50% of your Social

Security benefits added to your taxable income. If your combined income exceeds these thresholds, expect 85% of your Social Security benefits added to your taxable income. If your combined income is less than these thresholds, you won't be taxed on your Social Security benefits.

Here's an example of how this works:

Maggie collects Social Security benefits of $35,000, and she has an additional income of $20,000 and nontaxable interest of $1,000. When she goes to file her taxes, her combined income is $20,000 + $1000 + (0.5 x $35,000) = $38,500. According to the IRS, up to 85% of this may be taxed. So $38,500 x 0.85 = $32,725 is taxable income at the federal level.

To lower her tax obligation, Maggie will need to take into account deductions and credits allowed by the IRS.

State Taxes: Yes, It Matters Where You Live

In 2024, there are ten states that tax Social Security benefits: Colorado, Connecticut, Kansas, Minnesota, Montana, New Mexico, Rhode Island, Utah, Vermont, and West Virginia.

However, certain states—namely Alaska, Washington, Nevada, South Dakota, Texas, Wyoming, and Florida—impose no state income tax. Consequently, they don't tax Social Security benefits or any other income at the state level.

So if you're planning to retire in a different state, moving to one that doesn't tax income or Social Security could be a wise move that'll save you a lot of money.

Effective Ways to Drop Your Tax Bills in Retirement

When it comes to lowering your tax obligations post-career, there are several strategies to consider. These include converting traditional retirement savings to Roth IRAs, making smart withdrawals from different accounts, delaying Social Security for better benefits, and selling investments wisely. Also, being aware of available tax credits and deductions, using tax-efficient investment locations, and exploring options like qualified charitable distributions and health savings accounts can play a significant role.

Withdrawal Strategies That Lessen Your Tax Liability

As you begin to draw from your retirement accounts, you may be stuck with a tax bill. There are methods to reduce that tax obligation through strategic withdrawal plans, as described below. **You can opt to:**

- Convert your traditional retirement plans to a Roth IRA.

- Aim for a balanced approach by withdrawing from both taxable and tax-deferred accounts.

- Delay initiating Social Security benefits.

- Sell investments with long-term capital gains to provide income while enjoying lower tax rates.

- Take advantage of available credits and deductions, such as the Senior Tax Credit, medical expense deductions, and property tax credits.

- Spread large withdrawals over several years.

- Donate to charities through a variety of different strategies.

- Sell investments that have experienced a loss.

A tax or retirement professional can look at your accounts as a whole and advise where you can make adjustments to minimize your tax bill.

Roth Conversions: A Smart Tool for Tax-Free Income

Roth IRAs are popular because they're funded with after-tax dollars. As your money grows, it grows tax-free, so by the time you're ready to take the money out and use it in retirement, it may have grown into a sizable amount.

It's possible to convert funds from a traditional IRA or a qualified employer-sponsored retirement plan—a 401(k)—to a Roth IRA. Taxes will be due on the amount you convert in the following tax year, but after the conversion, your funds will grow tax-free.

Here's how the conversion typically works:

1. First, ensure that your plan qualifies for a conversion. A retirement professional or the fund manager should be able to help you with this.

2. Decide how much you want to convert. You can convert the entire balance of your IRA or just a portion, but bear in mind that the more you convert, the more taxes you may need to pay.

3. Contact a brokerage or your financial institution for the proper process and necessary forms.

4. Decide what type of conversion you'll initiate. A direct conversion transfers the money directly from the IRA to the Roth IRA without you taking possession of the money. In an indirect conversion, the funds are transferred to you, and you have a 60-day window to deposit them into the Roth IRA without facing penalties or fees.

5. The safest way to transfer funds is direct conversion.

6. Set aside funds outside of the IRA to pay the tax liability.

Since there's still a tax burden, you'll want to do careful calculations and consult with a tax professional.

If you're wondering about the optimal time for a Roth conversion, **let's look at a few scenarios in which it might make sense:**

- During years when your taxable income is lower than usual. This could be during a period of unemployment, sabbatical, or early retirement before Social Security or RMDs kick in.

- During market downturns when the value of your portfolio is lower. This allows you to pay taxes on a smaller account balance, and when the market rebounds, the appreciation in the Roth IRA is tax-free.

- When you have the money to cover the taxes using funds from accounts other than the IRA.

- Before changes in tax laws that could affect the taxation of retirement accounts.

Required Minimum Distributions (RMDs)

Individuals must make mandatory withdrawals from their tax-deferred retirement accounts once they turn a certain age (73 in 2024). The goal of RMDs is to ensure that retirement savings are used for income during retirement rather than letting the funds grow tax-deferred indefinitely.

RMDs must be taken from traditional IRAs, 401(k)s, 403(b)s, 457(b)s, and similar retirement plans. The amount of the RMD is calculated based on life expectancy and the account balance at the end of the previous year. [7] If you fail to withdraw the RMD, the IRS charges penalties of up to 50% of the distribution.

Let's look at an example. Ginny turned 72 in 2023. She must start taking RMDs in 2024 (the year she turns 73), and she's required to take them by April 1, 2025. If she fails to take the RMD, the amount she fails to withdraw can be taxed as high as 50%. Ginny talks to her financial planner and decides that, while she doesn't need the money, she could place it in a savings account or donate some to charity.

Winning at Charitable Giving

Donating to charities in your retirement can be a fulfilling and impactful way to support causes near to your heart, **and there are a few ways to do this:**

- Donor-advised funds (DAFs) enable you to contribute to a charitable cause, get an instant tax deduction, and later suggest grants from the fund. This allows you to support multiple charities through a single fund.

- Withdrawals directly made from your IRA to eligible charities are known as qualified charitable distributions (QCDs). If you're 73 or older, this can fulfill your RMD.

- Charitable remainder trusts (CRTs) and charitable lead trusts (CLTs) entail establishing a trust to generate income for either the donor or the charity for a specified period. Upon the trust's conclusion, the remaining assets are allocated to the designated beneficiaries or charities.

- To lessen your tax burden, you might also consider donating appreciated securities or other assets. By not selling the asset yourself, you steer clear of incurring capital gains taxes that would have otherwise been applicable.

- In addition to donating money during your lifetime, you can also support charities with your time and skills through volunteering.

- You can also include charitable giving in your bill or estate plan.

Estate Tax: Planning for Your Heirs

The last thing you want to do is leave your heirs with a big mess when they inherit your estate. **That's why it's crucial to outline what's included, which might be:**

- Land, as well as buildings or structures on that land

- Personal possessions such as furniture, jewelry, vehicles, or other tangible items

- Financial assets like bank accounts, investments, retirement accounts, and other financial holdings

- Debts and liabilities, including any financial obligations you may have

A failure to be thorough in listing the contents of your estate may result in a lengthy time in probate court and an unintended tax burden—not exactly the legacy you'd like to be remembered by. You're thinking that you're setting your heirs up for comfort, and they end up saddled with complications. Effective planning can guarantee a seamless transfer of your assets.

Understanding the Federal Estate Tax

The US government imposes the federal estate tax on the transfer of a deceased person's estate to their heirs. This tax is levied on the entire estate value—encompassing money, property, and other assets—surpassing a specified threshold called the estate tax exemption. In 2024, the exemption is $13.61 million for individuals and $27.22 million for married couples. Estates exceeding this threshold face a tax rate ranging from 18% to 40% on the amount surpassing the exemption.

It's important to note that these exemption rates are temporary and are set to drop down to between $5 million and $6 million in 2026.

The main goal of the federal estate tax is to generate government revenue and prevent the accumulation of wealth within a limited number of families.

The Cost of Death: State Inheritance & Estate Taxes

In addition to the federal estate tax, many states impose their own estate or inheritance taxes. These state-level taxes vary, with some applying to the entire estate and others only to amounts exceeding specific thresholds. Understanding your state's tax laws is essential for effective estate planning, as they can significantly impact the overall tax liability on your estate.

There are 13 states that don't tax 401(k), IRA, or pension distributions: Washington, Nevada, Alaska, Wyoming, South Dakota, Iowa, Illinois, Tennessee, Texas, Mississippi, Florida, Pennsylvania, and New Hampshire.

Two states tax 401(k) and IRA distributions but not pensions: Alabama and Hawaii.

Ways You Can Minimize Your Estate Taxes

Numerous strategies exist to reduce estate taxes and optimize the assets passed on to your heirs:

- Make gifts to individuals without triggering gift taxes. For 2024, the amount is $18,000 per person, and your spouse can also give that amount.

- Using trusts can reduce the taxable value of your estate.

- Married couples can transfer money to each other tax-free.

- Transfer assets to your surviving spouse, also tax-free.

For tailored guidance in your particular circumstances, seek advice from financial advisors, estate planning attorneys, and tax professionals.

The SECURE Act and the Ten-Year Rule

The SECURE Act, which went into law in December of 2019, **changed how you must handle retirement savings in a number of ways [8]:**

- It increased the age for RMDs to 72.

- It removed the age limit for contributing money to an IRA. You can contribute to an IRA as long as you've earned income.

- It made it easier for small businesses to offer retirement plans to their employees.

- It offered penalty-free withdrawals for the birth or adoption of a child.

- It created the ten-year rule, whereby heirs (other than spouses) must withdraw the inheritance housed in an IRA within ten years of the original owner's death.

This last provision is one that your heirs must be aware of. Before the SECURE Act, heirs had the option to stretch out their withdrawals over their lifetime. The "stretch-IRA" strategy allowed beneficiaries to take smaller RMDs annually based on their life expectancy. Because of this act, that time has been shortened to ten years and is referred to as the "IRA ten-year rule."

The new rule allows beneficiaries to withdraw the balance all at once or a little at a time—just as long as it's *all* removed by the end of the ten-year period.

However, there are exceptions to this rule. Surviving spouses, minor children, disabled individuals, and those not more than ten years younger than the deceased account owner may still have the option to stretch out the withdrawals based on their life expectancies. Contact a retirement professional for details.

Key Takeaways

- To maximize your retirement income, take the time to understand your tax situation. Analyze your income sources and distributions.

- Different types of income are taxed in different ways.

- Social Security benefits may be taxed up to 85% based on your combined income.

- Not all states tax distributions, so if you're considering a move, think about relocating to a tax-friendlier part of the country.

- Effective retirement planning involves strategies such as conversion to Roth IRAs, making strategic withdrawals, delaying Social Security benefits, and using tax credits and deductions.

- While you must withdraw RMDs when you reach a certain age, you have options with what to do with that money that can save you on taxes.

- Charitable giving allows you to support causes while reducing your tax burden.

- Estate planning will save your heirs time and money—and reduce the estate and state tax burdens as well.

Do you want help correctly planning your retirement and your estate, and minimizing your taxes for both along the way?
That's why we created our Retirement Planning Toolkit.

The Toolkit shows you:

- A step-by-step checklist for your retirement plan, so you can maximize your savings and avoid any costly pitfalls.

- An exact checklist for each phase of the estate planning process, so you leave no stone unturned and make sure you're fully prepared to protect your heirs and leave a legacy.

- How to minimize your taxes in retirement so you can preserve wealth, maximize income, and achieve your financial goals.

To download it, just go to Monroemethod.com/retirement-plan **or scan the QR code below:**

Chapter 5

Tackling Health Care Costs As You Age

"Retirement is like a long vacation in Las Vegas. The goal is to enjoy it to the fullest, but not so fully that you run out of money."

-Jonathan Clements, British author and scriptwriter

As they approach or settle into their retirement years, one of the most pressing concerns for many people is how to manage healthcare costs. Sure, you may feel healthy now, but who knows what'll happen in the future? Your mother lived to be 90, but your father had heart problems in his 70s. You just don't know.

With medical expenses often rising as we age, it's important to understand the options available to ensure that your health and finances remain in good shape.

Too often, people retire for health reasons and spend their retirement years seeing doctors and managing complex issues—not exactly ideal. Some retirees are healthy for a period of time but then age takes its toll. If we had a crystal ball, planning would be so much easier. But we don't.

Let's consider an example. Mary is in her early 80s, and her husband passed away a few years ago after suffering from an incurable disease for 20 years of his retirement. They enjoyed several years of travel before she became his primary caregiver. After he passed, she rethought her retirement plans and settled into a routine of volunteer work and single living, but suddenly she had a stroke. Luckily, it was fairly minor but it still affected her vision. Her daughter moved in to care for Mary while she decided what the rest of her life would look like. She figured that her life expectancy (judging by her family's longevity) would be another 15 years or so. Mary is lucky, as her husband left her in good financial shape with excellent health insurance. Others, however, aren't so lucky.

In this chapter, we'll explore the strategies and tools you can utilize to navigate the complex landscape of healthcare in your golden years.

Financial Basics of Health Care During Retirement

If you worked a full-time job before retirement, you probably had a health insurance plan that was fully or partially covered by your employer. But now you'll need to rely on an individual plan, or a combination of Medicare, supplemental insurance, and personal savings to cover your healthcare costs. [9]

Retirees have quite a few choices for health insurance coverage:

- **Medicare** is a federal health insurance program designed for people age 65 and older.

- **Medigap** covers expenses not covered by Medicare, including copayments, coinsurance, and deductibles.

- Some **employers** offer retiree health benefits as part of their retirement package, and may include coverage to supplement Medicare or provide primary coverage.

- **COBRA** (Consolidated Omnibus Budget Reconciliation Act) allows employees to continue their employer-sponsored plan if they pay the full premium.

- The **Health Insurance Marketplace** offers individual health insurance plans if you don't yet qualify for Medicare or Medicaid.

- If your **spouse** isn't retired, you may be able to join their employer's health insurance plan.

- **HRAs (health reimbursement arrangements) or HSAs (health savings accounts)** can be funded by employers and/or retirees to cover out-of-pocket medical expenses.

- **VA (Veterans Administration)** benefits are available to veterans based on their service history or disability status.

Understanding Medicare

Medicare serves as the cornerstone of health care coverage for Americans aged 65 and older, who are US citizens or permanent legal residents, and who've lived in the US for at least five continuous years. You may also qualify for Medicare if you're younger than 65 and have a qualifying disability or end-stage renal disease.

Medicare consists of four parts, each addressing distinct aspects of healthcare services.

- **Part A—Hospital Insurance:** Typically covers services related to stays in a facility or home health care.

  - Hospital stays encompass semi-private rooms, meals, general nursing, and additional services and supplies

- ○ Following a hospital stay, skilled nursing facility care is available for a limited time

- ○ Those with terminal illnesses can use home hospice care, which includes pain relief management and supportive services

- ○ Home health care services include skilled nursing care, physical or occupational therapy, and speech-language pathology services, among others

- **Part B—Medical Insurance:** Encompasses medically essential services and preventive care.

  - ○ Doctor's visits with your primary care physician, specialist, or other healthcare providers

  - ○ Outpatient services such as diagnostic tests, lab services, and outpatient surgeries

  - ○ Durable medical equipment, including wheelchairs, walkers, and oxygen equipment

  - ○ Preventative services such as screenings for cancer, cardiovascular disease, diabetes, and other conditions

  - ○ Vaccines such as flu and pneumococcal shots

- **Part C—Medicare Advantage:** Plans sanctioned by Medicare but administered through private healthcare companies. These plans offer all the benefits of Parts A and B and frequently include prescription drug coverage (Part D), along with extra benefits like dental and vision care.

- **Part D—Prescription Drug Coverage:** Assists in the costs associated with medications prescribed by your doctor. There are different plans to choose from, so pick one based on coverage, formularies, premiums, deductibles, and copayments.

To apply for Medicare, contact the Social Security Administration online or in person. You have the option to enroll up to three months before or three months after the birthday month that you turn 65. If you miss this enrollment period, you could be assessed penalties or experience gaps in insurance coverage.

Filling the Gaps with Medigap & Medicare Advantage Plans

Although Original Medicare (Parts A and B) offers extensive coverage for numerous healthcare services, it doesn't cover all expenses, including copayments, coinsurance, and deductibles.

To address these gaps, retirees have the option to choose between Medigap (Medicare Supplement Insurance) plans and Medicare Advantage plans.

Medigap plans, available from private insurance companies, require a monthly premium. They offer a variety of options, each with its own unique benefits. These plans help cover expenses that would otherwise be out of pocket. To qualify for Medigap coverage, enrollment in Medicare Parts A and B is required.

Medicare Advantage plans, also known as Medicare Part C, are obtained through private insurance companies. These plans provide additional benefits such as prescription drug coverage (Part D), as well as dental, vision, hearing, and fitness benefits. While Medicare Advantage plans typically have lower out-of-pocket expenses, accessing services often requires seeing providers within their network.

When choosing between Medigap and Medicare Advantage plans, it's important to weigh factors such as cost, coverage requirements, provider options, and flexibility. Medigap plans may offer more flexibility in provider choice and fewer out-of-pocket costs for beneficiaries who require frequent healthcare services. On the other hand, Medicare Advantage plans may provide additional benefits and cost-saving opportunities but with potential limitations on provider networks. Ultimately, compare the options available in your area and choose the plan that best meets your individual healthcare needs and budget.

Anticipating the Possibility of Long-Term Care

Aimed at addressing your health and personal care needs when you're unable to independently perform activities of daily living, long-term care encompasses various services. This may involve aid with tasks like bathing, dressing, eating, and mobility, as well as medical care administered in settings such as nursing homes, assisted living facilities, or at home by a caregiver.

Your health status and risk factors such as age, chronic health conditions, family history, and lifestyle factors may impact your future care needs. Even if you're feeling shiny and healthy right now, circumstances can change and you need to be prepared.

Let's consider George, who lives on a small farm. Until a few years ago, he tended cattle and cultivated a sizable garden. His wife is in fairly good health, but George has been having trouble with his back, which has restricted his mobility. Their son, who lives nearby, took over the majority of the outdoor chores. George also has chronic high blood pressure and the doctors are concerned about his heart. He wants to stay in his home but knows that it would put a burden on his wife as his caregiver. George and his wife have some savings they can use, but they need to make a plan for the future.

The following are some factors that they need to look at:

- The costs of home health care services and the availability of those services in their small town

- Types of long-term care insurance including coverage limits, benefit periods, elimination periods, inflation protection, and premiums

- Alternative sources of coverage for care expenses including annuities, reverse mortgages, Medicaid planning, and other assets

George and his wife decide to sit down and make their wishes clear to each other, including the possibility that George's wife might not be able to care for her husband and the homestead. They decide to make an appointment with a financial advisor to determine how long-term care fits into their budget.

Keeping Your Wallet Healthy (Even If You're Not)

It's a no brainer, but let's emphasize here that the quality of your life in retirement depends on your health as well as the health of your finances. As you age, you want to ensure that your financial well-being can cover the possibility that you may face health challenges down the road (or even sooner than that). Let's explore some things that you can do to keep your wallet healthy, even if you're not feeling your best.

- Regularly review your financial situation, including budgeting, saving, and investing to identify any areas that may lead to larger financial problems in the coming years.

- Create an emergency fund to address unexpected medical expenses or home repairs. A common recommendation is to save three to six months' worth of living expenses in an easily accessible savings account.

- Explore insurance options to protect your finances in case of unforeseen events. These include health, life, and long-term care insurance.

- If you haven't yet retired, continue to contribute to retirement accounts and pay down your debt.

- Seek advice from a financial professional to ensure that you're making progress toward your goals.

Health Savings Accounts (HSAs): The Triple Tax Advantage Option

HSAs offer a triple tax advantage that can result in significant cost savings. These accounts are meant to help cover medical expenses that aren't covered in high-deductible health plans (HDHPs). **Let's dig into the triple tax advantages of HSAs:**

1. HSAs are funded with **pre-tax dollars**, lowering the amount of income on your tax returns.

2. HSA funds provide **tax-free growth** while in the HSA account. You can choose a diversified portfolio of stocks, bonds, and other investments.

3. Withdrawals are **tax-free** when used with qualified expenses. You can use HSA funds for doctor visits, prescription medications, hospital stays, dental care, vision care, and certain over-the-counter items. By utilizing HSA funds to cover eligible medical expenses, you can effectively sidestep taxes on the withdrawn money, thereby maximizing the value of your healthcare dollars.

An HSA is a valuable resource for future healthcare needs, but make sure that you understand eligibility requirements, contributions, and rules regarding withdrawals to make the most of this tool.

Managing Dental Care Expenses

This is an important aspect of overall healthcare planning, as dental health plays a significant role in your overall well-being. While dental care is often overlooked, neglecting it can lead to serious health issues and costly treatments down the line. **Below are some strategies for managing dental care expenses effectively:**

- We're not trying to sound like your mother here, but brush and floss. Maintaining good dental hygiene can help minimize the likelihood of developing dental issues that might lead to expensive treatments.

- See your dentist regularly for maintenance and to prevent bigger problems.

- Purchase dental insurance. Medicare offers limited coverage but may not cover routine cleanings, exams, fillings, or extractions.

- An HSA can be used to cover dental care tax-free.

- Dental offices often provide payment plans or financing options if the bill doesn't fit your budget. If dental care is still too expensive, search for low-cost or free dental care options from health clinics, dental schools, or non-profit organizations.

Pros & Cons of Buying Long-Term Care Insurance

This type of insurance covers the costs of services like nursing home care, assisted living, and home health care. While long-term care insurance can offer valuable financial security, it's crucial to carefully evaluate the advantages and downsides before deciding to purchase a policy. [10]

Pros:

- Can provide financial security by helping to cover the substantial costs associated with long-term care services

- Offers more options and control over the type of care you receive and the provider

- Offers peace of mind and prevents burdening loved ones with financial costs

- Premiums may be tax-deductible

Cons:

- It can be expensive, and premiums often increase as you age

- Policies can be hard to understand with various options, features, and limitations

- Pre-existing conditions and health issues may disqualify you from receiving coverage or result in higher premiums

- Premium rate increases are common

- You can't recover the cost of your premiums if you never use the coverage

- The benefits can be limited based on the plan

Assessing the pros and cons of long-term care insurance involves weighing factors like coverage benefits, premium costs, and potential limitations. While it can provide financial security and peace of mind, it may not be suitable for everyone due to its expense and eligibility requirements. Alternative options for financing long-term care needs include self-funding, Medicaid planning, or exploring other insurance products like hybrid life insurance policies with long-term care benefits.

It's crucial to assess each option based on personal circumstances and preferences to make an informed decision, considering both benefits and drawbacks. Consulting with a financial advisor or insurance specialist can help you decide whether insurance is the best choice and, if yes, help you choose the best coverage for your needs.

Getting Familiar with the Medicaid Safety Net

Medicaid serves as a vital fallback for millions of Americans, providing access to healthcare coverage for low-income individuals and families who may otherwise be unable to afford medical care. Here's a brief overview of how Medicaid works.

- **Medicaid eligibility varies from state to state and hinges on a variety of factors:**
  - Generally, you must be between 60 and 62 (depending on the state requirement)
  - Income limits are also determined by the state and are typically calculated as a percentage of the federal poverty level

- o Medicard considers your assets in their calculation, which includes your primary residence and personal belongings

- o Some states may require elderly individuals to show a functional need for long-term care services, such as help with daily activities like bathing or managing medications

- o You must be a US citizen, national, or qualified immigrant meeting specific residency requirements

- o Most Medicaid recipients are also enrolled in Medicare

- Medicaid covers services such as doctor visits, preventive care, hospital stays, prescription medications, mental health services, and long-term care.

- Check with your state for specific requirements. As a result of the Affordable Care Act (ACA), more adults with higher incomes may be eligible.

- Applicants should apply through the state Medicaid agency and be prepared to provide the proof of eligibility listed above.

- A managed care organization is a private health insurance company that provides coverage to Medicaid recipients. They may also offer additional services for wellness management or disease prevention.

If you qualify for Medicaid, it can definitely provide a safety net when dealing with health issues. If you don't qualify, a financial professional can discuss asset transfers, spend-down strategies, and the use of trusts to help you meet the eligibility requirements.

Key Takeaways

- Consider your health situation when planning for retirement, including options for health insurance.

- There are four Medicare plans, each addressing distinct aspects of healthcare services.

- Medigap and Medicare Advantage can cover gaps in coverage left by Medicare plans.

- Prepare for the potential need for long-term care services, which may include considering long-term care insurance policies.

- Health Savings Accounts offer triple tax advantages that can provide significant benefits for covering medical expenses in retirement.

- Don't neglect your teeth in retirement—explore your options for dental care.

- Long-term care insurance has both advantages and disadvantages, and it's important to thoroughly assess these factors before deciding to purchase a policy.

- Medicaid can serve as an essential safety net for those with a lower income.

Chapter 6

Livin' Large: Your Retirement Housing Options

"Twenty years from now, you will be more disappointed by the things you didn't do than by the ones you did do. So throw off the bowlines. Sail away from the safe harbor. Catch the trade winds in your sails. Explore. Dream. Discover."
-from P.S. I Love You by author H. Jackson Brown

Let's consider Lyla's situation. When she decided to quit her job, she knew that she wasn't ready to settle for the quiet life just yet. Lyla had always been a bit of a wanderer—she'd traveled to some incredible places over the years, and a couple of them seemed like perfect spots to put down roots.

But there was one thing weighing on her mind: her retirement dollars. Lyla knew that her money would stretch a lot further in other countries than it would back home in the states. So before she retired, she took matters into her own hands and started downsizing.

She sold her home and let go of many of her belongings, clearing the way for a fresh start. Then, armed with a sense of adventure and a desire for a simpler life, she began researching potential destinations.

In the end, Lyla found herself drawn to Mexico. The low cost of living, the ease of life as an expatriate, and her grasp of Spanish (albeit basic) made it an ideal choice. She eventually took the plunge and made the move south of the border.

But Lyla didn't stop there. With her newfound freedom, she decided to turn her passion for living abroad into a business. She set up an online consultancy helping others navigate the ins and outs of retiring outside of the United States. It not only occupied her time but kept her engaged with a network of friends.

When you think about *your* retirement, where do you see yourself? Are you content to stay put in your current home, surrounded by familiar comforts? Or maybe you dream of packing it all in and hitting the road in an RV? Perhaps even setting sail on a boat to shores you've always dreamt about?

Or like Lyla, maybe you're drawn to the idea of starting a new chapter in a foreign land, soaking up the sun in Mexico, Portugal, or Spain. Whatever your vision for retirement, this chapter will explore the different options available, from staying put to downsizing, relocating abroad, or exploring senior living communities. And along the way, we'll dive into the financial considerations that come with each choice, from the costs of aging in place to the complexities of reverse mortgages.

Considering Where To Live in Retirement: Should You Leave the USA?

One of the fantastic things about retirement (and there are many) is that we finally have the time to do the things we've always wanted to, including venturing abroad and maybe even setting down roots there. But not all of us have dreams of Tuscan villas or Spanish seas—sometimes home is right where you've always known it to be. Let's delve into what your retirement might look like if you decide to stay put, along with the necessary adjustments you'll likely need to make.

Remaining at Home: Making the Necessary Safety Modifications

Staying in your current home likely holds sentimental value and familiarity, but as you age, you may need to consider some safety modifications. **These might include:**

- Installing grab bars in the bathroom (near the toilet, bathtub, and shower) can provide stability and support.

- Upgrading bathroom fixtures, such as a raised toilet seat, walk-in shower, and a handheld showerhead.

- Placing non-slip mats or strips in the bottom of the tub.

- Improving lighting in darker areas such as hallways, staircases, and entryways. Motion sensor lights can light pathways automatically.

- Removing trip hazards such as clutter, loose rugs, and electrical cords. You want to make sure that there's enough space to walk through all areas.

- Installing handrails on staircases for extra support.

- Adjusting kitchen features, such as lowering countertops, cabinets, and appliances to make them more accessible and easier to stand or sit next to when preparing meals. Also, lever-style handles on the faucet and cabinets are easier to grasp.

- Making sure that your flooring materials aren't a slip hazard, especially when they become wet from spills.

- Taking advantage of technology advancements such as smart-home devices, voice-controlled assistants, and smart thermostats—these provide a more accessible home environment for older adults.

Senior centers and non-profit agencies employ occupational therapists who can provide suggestions based on your needs. Remember that these modifications and devices aren't meant to remind you of what you can't do—they're intended to help you adapt to your changing needs and enable you to stay in your home.

Downsizing: Less Space, More Freedom?

Instead of staying in your current dwelling, you may be contemplating moving into something smaller that perhaps requires less yard work and upkeep.

Downsizing is all about moving from a larger house to something smaller and more manageable. It might sound a bit scary at first—getting rid of many of your beloved items and squeezing everything else into a smaller space—but this is all in the name of gaining freedom and flexibility.

You've spent years accumulating possessions, gifts, and all kinds of, well, clutter, and so downsizing offers an opportunity to decompress, offload unnecessary items, and streamline your living space. In fact, some people believe that less clutter means less stress, and it makes sense when you think about it.

In addition, downsizing can actually save you money. Smaller homes usually come with lower bills in terms of mortgage, utilities, and maintenance. So not only are you freeing up space but you're also freeing up your finances to spend on the things you love, like travel or new hobbies now that you're retired. Downsizing can also unlock home equity, providing you with extra income and less worry.

And then there's the inevitable emotional aspect. Downsizing requires letting go of sentimental attachments to belongings and embracing a more minimalist mindset. While parting with cherished items may initially evoke feelings of nostalgia or loss, you may find that the sense of liberation and freedom that comes with downsizing outweighs any temporary discomfort. By focusing on the positive aspects of downsizing—increased mobility, reduced stress, and enhanced financial security, for example—you can embrace this transition as an opportunity for personal growth and renewal.

Furthermore, downsizing offers the opportunity for a new beginning. It allows you to reimagine your living space and create a home that better reflects your current lifestyle and needs. Whether it's moving closer to family, moving to a condominium in a vibrant urban neighborhood, or relocating to a retirement community, downsizing opens the door to new possibilities and experiences.

Retiring in Mexico (& Other Countries)

Moving to another country is becoming somewhat of a trend for retirees, and for good reason. Mexico offers a fantastic quality of life at a fraction of the cost compared to many places in the United States. Take a place like Mexico City, for example. It's a vibrant metropolis bursting with culture, history, and endless things to explore. And an enormous advantage is that your dollar stretches much further here. You can enjoy delicious meals, cultural events, and entertainment without breaking the bank.[11] The best neighborhoods to consider in Mexico City for retirees are Condesa, Roma (Norte and Sur),

Polanco, and Coyoacan—all of which offer lush park and greenery, great restaurants, and a relaxing (and safe) lifestyle.

Then there's Merida, a charming colonial city known for its relaxed pace and warm, welcoming locals. It's an ideal destination to bask in the sun and fully experience Mexican culture. Or San Miguel de Allende, with its cobblestone streets, eye-catching buildings, and lively expat community—many find it a fabulous place to spend retirement.

Regarding cost of living, Mexico is considerably more affordable than many places in the United States. You'll find that everything from housing to groceries to healthcare is more cost-effective, allowing you to stretch your retirement savings further and enjoy a higher standard of living.

But Mexico isn't the only option for retirees seeking to enjoy their golden years in a foreign land. Countries like Portugal and Spain also provide fantastic opportunities for expatriates. Portugal, boasting a breathtaking coastline, captivating history, and welcoming locals, is witnessing a surge in popularity among retirees. Spain, renowned for its sunny weather, diverse culture, and exceptional healthcare system, stands as another prime destination for expats contemplating retirement abroad.

Whether you're dreaming of sipping margaritas on a beach in Mexico, exploring cobblestone streets in Portugal, soaking up the sun in Spain, or relocating to somewhere we haven't mentioned, there's a world of possibilities waiting for you.

Assessing the Wide Variety of Senior Living Communities

As mentioned earlier, sometimes home is where the heart is, even if that home becomes a senior living community. There's a wide variety of these options available, so let's break them down and learn a little about what they have to offer.

Independent Living Communities

These are perfect for those who maintain an active and independent lifestyle but desire the ease of maintenance-free living, as well as access to amenities like fitness centers, social activities, and dining options. Independent living communities typically feature apartment-style homes or cottages, and they encourage a strong sense of community among residents.

Assisted Living Facilities

These communities offer increased care and support for seniors requiring assistance with their daily activities. Assisted living facilities commonly provide private or semi-private accommodations, tailored care plans, and round-the-clock access to trained staff assistance. Residents can also utilize communal spaces for socializing and participating in activities.

Memory Care Communities

Designed for older adults who require more specialized care due to medical conditions or impairments, these facilities are specifically designed to provide a safe and supportive environment for individuals with memory-related disorders, such as Alzheimer's or dementia. Memory care communities offer routine, specialized programs, as well as secure living spaces to promote residents' safety and well-being.

Continuing Care Retirement Communities (CCRCs)

These facilities offer living arrangements ranging from independent living to skilled nursing care, allowing residents to age in one place as their needs change. CCRCs typically offer varied housing options, on-site healthcare services, and amenities. This comprehensive approach to senior living gives residents peace of mind knowing that they can receive the care they need without having to relocate to a different facility as certain conditions progress.

Active Adult Communities

Designed for individuals seeking an active lifestyle, these communities frequently include amenities like golf courses, swimming pools, and clubhouses. Active adult facilities offer diverse housing options such as single-family homes, townhouses, or condominiums, and they encourage residents to pursue their interests and hobbies while fostering a sense of community.

When evaluating senior living communities, it's essential to consider factors like location, amenities, and the level of care available. Visiting various communities, speaking with current residents, and reviewing contracts and policies can assist in making a well-informed decision that matches your requirements and preferences.

What Will Your Abode Really Cost?

Understanding the True Costs of Aging in Place

The real costs of aging in your own home are something that many of us think about as we enter our golden years. We want to stay in the comfort of our own dwellings but know that there are financial considerations to keep in mind. **Here are some things to consider:**

- Making our homes safer and more accessible as we age is a priority. As mentioned earlier, you might need to install grab bars, ramps, or stairlifts, and maybe even remodel parts of your home like the bathroom or kitchen.

- Your home also ages alongside you, and so it starts to require more attention and care, from regular maintenance tasks to unexpected repairs. Regular upkeep such as landscaping, gutter cleaning, and HVAC maintenance can add up over time, as can major repairs or replacements for systems like plumbing, roofing, and appliances.

- Also covered previously, you may need help with daily tasks as you get older. Whether it's assistance with chores, personal care, or medical needs, the cost of in-home care can accumulate quickly. While some retirees may be able to rely on family members or unpaid caregivers for support, others will require professional assistance from home health aides or other healthcare providers. Costs can vary depending on the level of assistance and where you live.

- Healthcare costs are another big consideration. As we age, our medical needs will increase, from routine check-ups to prescription medications and everything in between. Factor in out-of-pocket expenses for healthcare services, deductibles, copayments, and premiums when planning for your retirement budget. Long-term care insurance may also be worth considering as a way to offset potential future expenses related to nursing home care or assisted living.

- The cost of living tends to go up over time, which means that our retirement savings might not stretch as far as we'd hoped due to inflation. Take time to look at your budget to make sure that it remains realistic and sustainable as the economy changes.

Aging in place offers many benefits, but it's essential to understand the true costs and financial implications associated with remaining in your home. By planning ahead, budgeting for potential expenses, and exploring the resources and support options available, you can take steps to ensure that you can age in place safely, comfortably, and affordably for years to come.

Selling Your Home: Capital Gains & Exclusions

Before you sign on the dotted line, let's explore t what selling your dwelling means for your finances, particularly when it comes to capital gains and exclusions.

When you sell your home, any profit from the sale is called a capital gain, which is the difference between the sale price and what you originally paid for the property, plus any improvements or renovations you've made over the years.

But here's where things get interesting: The IRS allows for certain exclusions on capital gains from the sale of your primary residence. Currently, if you've owned and lived in your home for at least two of the past five years, you might qualify to exclude up to $250,000 of capital gains from your taxable income. If you're married and filing jointly, that exclusion doubles to $500,000.

This can be a huge financial benefit for those looking to cash in on their home equity without facing a hefty tax bill. It's a way to reap the rewards of homeownership and potentially fund your retirement dreams without worrying about the government taking a big portion of your profits.

Additionally, there are limits on how often you can claim the exclusion (once every two years), as well as state tax considerations.

The bottom line is that the capital gains exclusion can be incredibly beneficial for individuals aiming to downsize, relocate, or tap into their home equity during retirement.

Renting vs. Buying: How They Affect Your Bank Account

The difference between buying and renting can have a profound impact on your bank account, especially in retirement when you're on a fixed income. Let's compare these two options below.

Renting

Renting generally involves lower initial expenses compared to purchasing a home. You'll typically pay a security deposit, as well as the first and last month's rent. Renting offers flexibility since you're not bound to a long-term mortgage agreement. However, rental payments can rise over time, and you won't accrue equity in the property. Consequently, renting might not be the most financially advantageous choice in the long term, particularly if property values increase.

Buying

Purchasing a home necessitates a substantial initial investment through a down payment, closing costs, and ongoing mortgage payments. Nevertheless, homeownership enables you to accumulate equity in the property over time, potentially yielding long-term financial advantages. Additionally, you have greater autonomy over your living environment and can personalize it to suit your preferences, and homeownership also provides tax benefits.

On the downside, homeowners are responsible for maintenance and repair expenses, property taxes, and homeowners insurance. These costs can accumulate over time and will vary depending on the property's condition.

Ultimately, the choice between renting and buying hinges on your financial circumstances, lifestyle preferences, and long-term objectives. Renting may be a more suitable option if you value flexibility and don't want to deal with the responsibilities of homeownership. Alternatively, buying a home can provide stability, equity buildup, and potential tax benefits, but it requires a larger upfront investment and ongoing financial commitment.

Before making a decision, consider factors such as your budget, future housing needs, and the real estate market in your area.

Reverse Mortgages: Do You Need One?

Considering a reverse mortgage can feel like a big step—after all, it's a way of utilizing your home's equity to address expenses during retirement. But before jumping in, it's crucial to think about the costs involved and how it might affect your family's future. Take time to explore other options, like downsizing or a home equity line of credit (HELOC), to determine what's best for you.

Although reverse mortgages can offer a valuable income source, they *do* come with certain risks and drawbacks. Before diving in, it's vital to understand the ins and outs of this option in terms of who's eligible, how repayment works, and any fees involved. [12]

Understanding How a Reverse Mortgage Works

A reverse mortgage permits homeowners aged 62 and older to access the equity they've accumulated in their homes without needing to sell the property.

With a reverse mortgage, the lender disburses payments to the homeowner, either as a lump sum, a line of credit, or in monthly installments. This sounds ideal, but it's a little more complicated than you might think.

First, you remain accountable for property taxes, insurance, and home maintenance expenses. Second, although you're not required to make monthly payments on the loan, the balance will progressively increase over time due to accruing interest. Consequently, the equity in your home will diminish, potentially affecting any inheritance that you intend to leave to your heirs.

Another aspect to consider is that reverse mortgages entail expenses such as closing costs, mortgage insurance premiums, and origination fees. These costs can diminish the amount of cash you receive from the loan, so it's essential to take them into account when deciding.

Despite the potential drawbacks, a reverse mortgage can serve as a valuable resource for individuals seeking to augment their income, address unforeseen expenses, or finance home improvements.

Reverse Mortgages: Pros & Cons

In addition to what's been briefly mentioned above, let's take a moment to examine in further detail the variety of benefits and disadvantages of reverse mortgages below.

Pros:

- A reverse mortgage offers older homeowners a means to access their home equity, providing a tax-free income source without needing to sell the property.

- You can choose to receive funds as a lump sum, a line of credit, or in monthly payments, allowing you to customize the loan to your specific financial requirements.

- You aren't obligated to make any payments as long as you continue to reside in the home.

- You can stay in your home while tapping into its equity, fostering a sense of stability and security during your retirement years.

Cons:

- Over time, the balance of a reverse mortgage grows due to accruing interest, diminishing the equity in your home and potentially affecting any inheritance you plan to leave to your heirs.

- Reverse mortgages entail fees such as closing costs, mortgage insurance premiums, and origination expenses, which can reduce the cash received from the loan.

- Because a reverse mortgage is a loan, it must be repaid when the homeowner sells the home, permanently relocates, or passes away. This could reduce the inheritance left to heirs and complicate the property ownership transfer process.

- Even though monthly payments aren't mandatory with a reverse mortgage, homeowners are still responsible for covering expenses such as property taxes, insurance, and home maintenance costs. Failing to fulfill these obligations could lead to default on the loan.

Alternatives to a Reverse Mortgage

If you're seeking options other than a reverse mortgage, several choices are available to tap into home equity without resorting to borrowing:

Home Equity Line of Credit (HELOC)

A HELOC is a flexible line of credit that enables homeowners to borrow against the equity in their home. With this option, homeowners can access funds as needed and make monthly payments on the borrowed amount. A home equity line of credit provides more flexibility in accessing funds and allows homeowners to borrow only what they need, potentially reducing interest costs.

Cash-Out Refinance

This entails refinancing your current mortgage for a sum greater than your existing loan balance, with the excess amount received in cash. A cash-out refinance allows homeowners to access a lump sum of cash while potentially securing a lower interest rate on their mortgage. However, it typically involves closing costs and may result in higher monthly mortgage payments.

Selling & Downsizing

Moving to a smaller, more affordable property can release cash while decreasing your housing expenses. This option allows homeowners to access their home equity in a lump sum and potentially eliminate mortgage payments altogether. Plus, it can also simplify maintenance, as well as reduce property taxes and insurance costs.

Rent Out a Portion of Your Home

Charging someone to live or stay in a spare bedroom or a basement apartment in your home can generate a consistent rental income without the need to incur debt or relinquish ownership of the property. This option allows homeowners to leverage their home's value while still retaining control over their living space.

Home Equity Conversion Mortgage (HECM) for Purchase

Homebuyers aged 62 or older can acquire a new home using a reverse mortgage, merging the advantages of homeownership with the flexibility of extra funds. It can be a valuable choice if you intend to downsize or relocate to a more suitable home during retirement.

Each of these alternatives presents distinct benefits and considerations, underscoring the importance of meticulously assessing your financial circumstances, objectives, and preferences before reaching a decision. Seek advice from a financial advisor or housing counselor to receive personalized guidance and assistance in determining the most suitable option for your needs.

Now let's consider the example of Ann and Jerry. This couple owns two homes—a primary residence and a smaller home on a lake a few hours away where they used to spend weekend getaways with their children. Now that their kids are grown, Jerry wants to spend more time fishing and Ann wants a simpler life. They're not sure whether they want to give up their primary residence, which is close to the city, and since both homes are paid off, they like the idea of holding onto the house in case one of their kids wants to move into it later on.

They decide to downsize to the smaller home because it's easier to take care of and more attuned to the lifestyle they desire. They make the choice to rent out their primary residence as an Airbnb, hiring a company to take care of the maintenance and rental details. Ann and Jerry can take heirlooms with them and store things they don't want to part with in a locked area of the house or off site. The rental fees will pay for the taxes and maintenance on the home until they decide what to do with it.

Deciding where you'll want to live out your retirement years will depend on countless factors, but as much as a Spanish hideaway or Mexican beach sound inviting (because they truly are), there are numerous considerations to ponder. Whether you choose to move abroad, modify your current residence, or ease into the idea of assisted living, the options require careful thought and planning so that your after-career existence is as enjoyable and cost-effective as possible.

Key Takeaways

- Investigate destinations where your money can go further, such as Mexico, Portugal, or Spain, for a higher quality of life at a lower cost.

- Downsizing isn't just about freeing up space—it's also about gaining freedom, flexibility, and financial savings while simplifying your life.

- If you choose to stay in your current home, make necessary safety modifications to ensure that it remains a safe and accessible environment as you age.

- Aging in place comes with financial considerations, including home modifications, maintenance, healthcare expenses, and potential inflation impacts.

- While reverse mortgages offer a source of income, it's crucial to weigh the pros and cons like accrued interest, fees, and impact on heirs before making a decision.

- Consider alternatives to reverse mortgages such as cash-out refinancing, downsizing, renting out a portion of your home, or utilizing a home equity conversion mortgage (HECM) for purchase.

Chapter 7

Maintaining Your Lifestyle: The Art of Spending Wisely in Retirement

"Retirement is like a long vacation in Las Vegas. The goal is to enjoy it to the fullest, but not so fully that you run out of money."
-Jonathan Clements, former reporter for The Wall Street Journal

What does "retirement" mean to you? Freedom from the daily grind? A permanent vacation from a grueling commute at 7:30 a.m.? Or maybe finally the opportunity to lay down residency in Mexico City, as we explored in our last chapter? While you wouldn't be incorrect if you chose any of the above, retirement ultimately means enjoying the life you've always wanted while making wise choices with your money.

Think of retirement as your chance to design the life you want. From tracking your spending to creating a budget that works for you, in this chapter we'll cover practical tips to help you make the most of your money in retirement.

We'll explore how to make your retirement funds last so that you can enjoy every moment to the fullest. We'll also dive into the concept of finding the right balance between enjoying yourself and being responsible. Whether you're dreaming of traveling the world or simply enjoying time with loved ones, we'll show you how to do it all without breaking the bank.

And when unexpected expenses pop up, like health bills or home repairs, we'll help you navigate them with confidence. Because in retirement, being prepared is key to peace of mind—no matter if you're in San Miguel de Allende or in San Francisco.

Crafting Your Personal Golden Years Game Plan

When charting your course for the decades ahead, begin by envisioning your perfect retirement. Would you like to travel, explore new interests, or enjoy more time with those who matter most? Next, assess your financial situation. Determine your current funds and the amount required to fulfill your dreams (and consider seeking guidance from a financial advisor if needed).

Here's the key: Be flexible. Your plans might change, and that's okay. The important thing is to stay focused on what matters to you. Remember—your retirement is yours to create. Whether you dream of quiet days at home or exciting adventures, make a plan that fits your desires so that you can truly enjoy your retirement.

Tracking Your Expenses for Fiscal Freedom

Keeping track of where your money goes is crucial for financial freedom in retirement. Start by documenting all your expenses, from groceries to leisure activities. This practice enables you to study your spending habits so that you can find ways to save money. Utilize tools such as budgeting apps or basic spreadsheets to effortlessly monitor your expenses. Establish a routine of regularly reviewing your spending to maintain control over your finances. Some popular budgeting apps to explore include Mint, YNAB (You Need a Budget), PocketGuard, Personal Capital, and Honeydue.

By knowing where your money goes, you can make smarter choices and have more control over your financial future—and that's a key ingredient in a satisfying and comfortable retirement.

Creating a Realistic & Sustainable Budget

Maintaining a budget that suits your needs is crucial for ensuring financial stability.

Document all sources of income such as pensions, Social Security, and withdrawals from savings, and then move onto identifying essential expenses like housing, healthcare, and groceries. Allocate a portion of your income to cover these essentials while also setting aside funds for discretionary spending on entertainment and travel. Be realistic about your spending habits and set achievable goals.

Regularly review and modify your budget to accommodate any changes in your financial circumstances or lifestyle. By crafting a budget that's both practical and enduring, you can savor your retirement without concerns about financial depletion.

Bending Your Budget Over Time

Your retirement budget should be flexible and adaptable. As you grow older, healthcare expenses will likely rise, and you might also opt to downsize your living arrangements. Be prepared to adjust your budget as your circumstances change.

Regularly reviewing your budget is essential to identifying areas where you need to make changes. Take into account shifts in income, expenses, and lifestyle preferences. Adjust your budget accordingly by reallocating funds between categories, renegotiating expenses like insurance premiums, or finding new ways to save money.

Stay focused on your long-term financial objectives while remaining open to unexpected expenses or opportunities that may arise. By being flexible with your budget, you can guarantee that your financial strategy remains in line with your changing requirements throughout retirement.

Smart Retirement Spending: The No-Scrooge Way

This section is all about striking a balance between enjoying life and being financially responsible without turning into a modern-day miser.

Start by prioritizing your spending based on what brings you joy. Focus on experiences and activities that enhance your quality of life—whether it's traveling, pursuing hobbies, or spending time with loved ones.

At the same time, be mindful of your budget and avoid overspending on unnecessary luxuries. Look for ways to make the most of your money such as seeking out discounts, shopping for sales, or taking advantage of rewards programs.[13]

Practice moderation when engaging in activities such as eating out, shopping, or other forms of entertainment. While it may be tricky at first to forego the frequent steak dinners you often enjoy, establish boundaries for yourself and adhere to them to prevent financial stress in the long run.

Finally, remember that being frugal doesn't mean being stingy. It's about making thoughtful choices that align with your values and priorities while still allowing yourself to enjoy life to the fullest. You can *still* enjoy that steak dinner or evening at the movies—just not every week. By practicing smart retirement spending, you can live comfortably and confidently without letting money rule your golden years.

Balancing Wants & Needs: Not As Painful As You Think

Retirement offers a unique chance to pursue your desires while also meeting your needs. Striking the right balance between the two can seem daunting, but it doesn't have to be that way.

Start by identifying your needs—the essential expenses crucial for your well-being and security, like housing, healthcare, groceries, and transportation. Once you've clarified these basic requirements, set aside a portion of your budget to cover them first.

Next, consider your wants—the non-essential purchases and experiences that bring joy and fulfillment such as travel, dining out, entertainment, and hobbies. While these may not be as vital as your needs, they're still important for a satisfying retirement.

Balancing wants and needs means prioritizing what matters most while being mindful of your financial situation. It's okay to treat yourself occasionally, but ensure that it aligns with your budget.

Seeing the World Without Breaking the Bank

Traveling is often high on the retirement bucket list, but it doesn't have to come at a high cost. With some savvy planning and a willingness to explore alternative options, you can see the world (or even the rest of your state if you crave adventure but prefer to stay closer to home) without breaking the bank.

- Begin by maintaining flexibility in your travel arrangements. Explore options like traveling during off-peak seasons or being receptive to last-minute deals. Utilize travel deal websites and apps to discover affordable flights, accommodations, and activities. They can be valuable resources for securing budget-friendly travel experiences.

- Look for cost-effective destinations where your dollar stretches further. Explore countries with lower living costs or opt for destinations that offer activities that are free or offered at reduced prices.

- Lodging options like vacation rentals, hostels, or house-swapping are frequently more budget-friendly than standard hotels and offer a more genuine travel experience. There's something really authentic and local about staying at a gorgeous Airbnb, for example.

- Set a daily budget for food, transportation, and activities, and always look for ways to save such as by cooking meals instead of dining out or using public transportation instead of taxis.

- Remember to utilize any travel rewards or loyalty programs you may be enrolled in. Whether it's using credit card points for flights or hotel stays or earning discounts through frequent traveler programs, every little bit helps when it comes to saving money on travel.

By being resourceful and creative with your travel plans, you can explore new sights and sensations without draining your well-earned retirement savings.

For example, Ron and Kathy both agreed that they wanted to travel in their retirement. They were both in good health and had worked hard to build a generous nest egg, but they were also aware that they had to follow a budget.

First, they sat down and figured out a yearly travel budget, and they decided that moving into a smaller home and selling an extra car and camper would free up more funds. Then came the fun part of brainstorming a bucket list of desired travel destinations—cruises in the Mediterranean and backpacking in the Andes topped their bucket list. They had a credit card that also gave them airline miles, so they funneled all their expenses through it, ensuring that they didn't go over budget on expenses so that they could pay the balance each month.

Then they did some extensive research. Instead of a luxury cruise, they found smaller ships that offered a more personalized experience. Instead of staying at ritzy hotels and dining out often, they explored the ideas of house-swapping and shopping at local markets for food. They loved the prospect of meeting new friends and learning the local culture. Ultimately, all these choices not only benefited their thrill-seeking, adventurous nature but were also kind to their wallets.

Cut the Costs, Keep the Fun

Retirement doesn't have to mean prohibitively tightening the purse strings—it's more about finding creative ways to enjoy life while staying within your means. By keeping an eye on your spending, you can cut costs without sacrificing the fun and enjoyment that retirement brings. Below, **some tips on how to set about doing this:**

- Carefully examine your expenses and pinpoint areas in which you can cut costs. This might involve renegotiating bills, canceling unused subscriptions, or seeking more cost-effective alternatives for your everyday purchases.

- Consider downsizing or decluttering your home to reduce maintenance and utility costs. Selling unused items can free up space and provide extra cash for fun activities or experiences.

- Look for free or low-cost ways to stay entertained and engaged in retirement. Explore local parks, museums, and community events, or take up hobbies that don't require a significant financial investment.

- Use senior discounts and special offers tailored for retirees to maximize savings. Many businesses offer discounted rates for seniors on everything from dining out to travel, so be sure to ask about available discounts wherever you go. There are perks to being a senior citizen, so take advantage of them!

- Keep in mind that the best things in life don't have to cost a fortune. Spending quality time with loved ones, enjoying nature, and pursuing passions and interests can bring immense joy and fulfillment without costing too many dimes.

Rolling with Retirement's Financial Punches

As mentioned quite a few times thus far, retirement is a journey filled with ups and downs, and it's important to be prepared for the unexpected financial challenges that may come your way. Whether it's unexpected home repairs or supporting loved ones, being prepared for whatever retirement might throw in your direction requires resilience and foresight.

Prepping for Major Home Repairs

While owning your own home in retirement can offer comfort and stability, it also entails the responsibility of maintaining and repairing it. Major home repairs can be costly and unexpected, so it's essential to be prepared and have a plan in place to address them.

Start by building an emergency fund for home repairs. It can provide comfort and ensure that you're financially prepared when unforeseen issues arise.

Inspections can help you catch signs of minor damage before they become bigger problems down the line. Consider scheduling routine maintenance checks for your home's systems and appliances to identify any issues before they become more serious.

Also, research financing options for significant home repairs, such as home equity lines of credit or personal loans. Talk to various lenders to determine the most suitable choice for your needs. Having access to financing can help cover the costs of major repairs without draining your savings.

In addition, explore investing in home warranty coverage to enhance protection against repair expenses. Home warranties typically cover significant systems and appliances within your home, offering assurances and financial protection in case of breakdowns or malfunctions.

Finally, don't underestimate the value of DIY projects and preventative measures to help maintain your home and reduce the risk of major repairs. Simple tasks like cleaning gutters, sealing cracks, and maintaining landscaping can help preserve your home's value and minimize the need for costly repairs. Not only that, but it's a great way to stay busy in your retirement years when the golf course or the pool have lost their luster. Shake things up by being handy around the house—it's great for exercise, a super workout for your mind, and your wallet won't complain either.

By taking a proactive approach to home maintenance and repair, you can prepare for major expenses and protect your retirement finances.

Helping Loved Ones While Protecting Your Assets

It's a bit inevitable, isn't it? Retirement may also bring requests for financial assistance from family members, whether it's helping a child with college tuition or supporting an aging parent. Balancing generosity with financial security is crucial, although it's natural to want to assist loved ones in need.

Begin by evaluating your financial situation and establishing a realistic amount that you can afford to contribute to assisting loved ones. Think about your retirement savings, income sources, and ongoing expenses before opening up your heart and your purse strings. [14]

Have open communications with your loved ones about your financial boundaries and limitations. Be honest about what you can and cannot afford to provide, and set clear expectations for any assistance that you're willing to offer. Promote open dialogue and collaboration to find solutions that satisfy everyone's needs while also respecting your financial limitations.

Also, explore alternative forms of support beyond direct financial assistance. This may involve providing more practical and hands-on help, such as offering childcare, transportation, or assistance with household chores. Additionally, consider sharing your knowledge and expertise to help loved ones develop financial literacy skills and budgeting strategies that can empower them to become more financially independent.

Protect your assets and retirement savings by setting up legal and financial safeguards. Consider establishing trusts, creating estate plans, or purchasing long-term care insurance to protect your assets and ensure they're used in accordance with your wishes. Work with a financial advisor or estate planning attorney to develop a comprehensive plan that addresses your specific needs and concerns.

Finally, prioritize your own financial well-being and retirement goals. While it's natural to want to support loved ones, it's essential to take care of your own needs first to avoid jeopardizing your own financial security. Remember that maintaining your own financial stability ultimately enables you to continue providing support to your loved ones in the long run.

For example, let's take Alice, who recently found herself in a tricky situation. She'd spent decades working hard, saving diligently, and dreaming of the days when she could live her retirement years in peace. However, retirement brought some unexpected family challenges—her son, Brian, was struggling to pay for his daughter's college tuition, and her mother was facing mounting medical expenses.

Alice spent time looking at her budget and wondering how she could help. She sat down with her son and mother and offered more than just financial assistance. She helped her son research scholarships and financial aid options, and she and her mother explored options for long-term care insurance. Alice prioritized her own needs while setting up trusts and an estate plan to care for her loved ones—and she didn't negatively affect her finances in the process.

Managing your money and knowing where it's going doesn't have to be a tricky aspect of your retirement—in fact, with the above tips and techniques, you can simplify the process to ensure that you're taken care of well after you punch the time clock for the final time.

Key Takeaways

- Crafting your retirement plan starts with envisioning your ideal lifestyle and assessing your financial situation.

- Flexibility is key in retirement budgeting. Be prepared to adjust your budget over time to accommodate your changing needs and circumstances.

- Balancing wants and needs in retirement involves prioritizing essential expenses while indulging in non-essential purchases that enhance your quality of life.

- Traveling in retirement can be affordable with careful planning. Be flexible with travel plans, explore budget-friendly destinations, and take advantage of discounts and rewards programs.

- Being prepared for unexpected financial challenges in retirement, such as health expenses and home repairs, involves building emergency funds, exploring insurance options, and staying proactive with budget adjustments and preventive measures.

Chapter 8

Making the Most of Your Retirement

"Living each day as if it were your last doesn't mean your last day of retirement on a remote island. It means to live fully, authentically and spontaneously with nothing being held back."

-Jack Canfield, co-author of the Chicken Soup for the Soul series

Let's consider Janice's scenario. She's retiring from a corporate job she's had for nearly 25 years, and like many others in her situation, she's looking forward to having some time for hobbies, seeing friends, and traveling. She's always wanted to take piano lessons and has found a great teacher at her local senior center. She's resolved to keep in touch with her work friends by scheduling lunch once a month. There's a local hiking club that meets on Tuesday mornings, and she's looking forward to checking it out for some exercise and to meet new folks.

Her daughter has also been pestering her to go through some photo albums and tell stories about her youth. And now that Janice thinks of it, she's sure that her daughter would love some family recipes that've been passed down for generations.

Retirement is a time that many think about as a period of simple relaxation, leisure, and freedom. The reality often far exceeds these expectations, presenting endless opportunities for growth, fulfillment, and meaningful contribution.

This chapter explores the ways you can make the most of your retirement years, ensuring that they shine bright with purpose, vitality, and joy.

Staying Brain Sharp and Body Spry

One of the key aspects of a successful retirement is staying savvy, both mentally and physically. **Below are some strategies to help you maintain your brain and your frame during your retirement:**

- **Stay Socially Connected**: Preserving strong social bonds is crucial for mental wellness during retirement. Frequent social engagements can help you feel less lonely and isolated.

- **Exercise Regularly**: This goes without saying, but physical activity is great for your overall health as you age. Incorporate a variety of exercises into your routine, including aerobic activities, strength training to maintain muscle mass, and flexibility exercises to increase your sense of balance. Set a goal to get at least 30 minutes of medium-intensity exercise each day.

- **Prioritize Sleep**: Quality shut-eye is essential for mental abilities, emotional balance, and general well-being. Establish a consistent bedtime routine, ensure a comfortable sleep environment, and refrain from stimulants like caffeine and electronic devices before bed. If you're experiencing sleep difficulties, seek advice from a healthcare professional if they persist.

- **Eat a Balanced Diet**: Maintaining proper nutrition is essential for sustaining health and vitality during retirement. Strive for a well-rounded diet abundant in whole foods, and keep hydrated by consuming ample water throughout the day. Also, as fun as they might be, cut back on processed foods, sugary snacks, and alcohol.

- **Challenge Your Brain:** Exercise your mind with things like crossword puzzles, Sudoku, brain teasers, and memory games—they're excellent ways to improve your brain health. Explore opportunities to acquire new skills or hobbies that demand mental focus and problem-solving capabilities.

- **Manage Stress:** Chronic anxiety and worry can negatively impact both your mental and physical well-being. Implement stress-reduction methods like mindfulness meditation, deep breathing exercises, or yoga to effectively manage stress levels. Also, engage in activities that bring joy and relaxation such as getting outside in nature, pursuing creative interests, or moments for self-care.

Exercising for Physical Strength

Physical exercise isn't just about maintaining a youthful appearance—it's also about ensuring that your body remains strong and capable of enjoying all the activities you have planned for your retirement. [15] Whether it's walking, swimming, yoga, or dancing, find an exercise routine that you enjoy and that fits your abilities. These activities will build your endurance and strength, but the important thing is to engage in them safely. **Keep these tips in mind when planning a strength routine:**

- **Start Slowly:** If you haven't been active for a while, take your time and increase the intensity of your workouts gradually.

- **Include Resistance Training:** Begin with light weights or resistance bands two or three times a week, and focus on proper form and technique to prevent injuries.

- **Balance and Stability Exercises:** Add activities such as single-leg balance, heel-to-toe walking, and stability ball exercises to your routine to build balance and ensure that you're always steady on your feet.

- **Include Rest and Recovery**: Take time to rest your muscles between workouts to prevent overtraining and minimize the risk of injury. On rest days, include stretching, foam rolling, or gentle yoga to promote flexibility and mobility.

A great way to keep your mind fresh and learn the proper moves is to take a class, find a video on the internet, join a gym, or hire a personal trainer. Staying active is the name of the aging game.

Lifelong Learning: Feed Your Brain

Retirement is the perfect time to indulge your curiosity and continue learning. Whether it's picking up a new language, taking up painting, or diving into topics you've always been interested in, lifelong learning keeps your mind engaged and vibrant.

Let's look at some ideas for discovering what makes you excited:

- **Explore New Subjects**: Whether it's history, art, science, literature, or philosophy, there are fascinating subjects waiting for you to dive into them.

- **Take Classes**: Many community colleges, universities, and online platforms offer a wide range of courses specifically designed for lifelong learners. Whether you lean toward traditional classroom environments or value the flexibility of online learning, there are options tailored to accommodate your preferences and schedule.

- **Attend Workshops and Seminars**: These events provide opportunities to learn from experts, engage in discussions with like-minded individuals, and stay up to date on current trends and developments in various fields.

- **Join Book Clubs**: Reading is a fantastic way to keep your mind sharp. Joining a book club can expand your perspectives and create social connections with fellow book lovers.

- **Engage in Discussions**: Whether it's with friends, family members, or members of a community group, engaging in thoughtful discussions on a wide range of topics can expand your horizons and challenge your perspectives.

- **Travel and Cultural Experiences**: Traveling allows you to experience new viewpoints and ways of life, providing invaluable opportunities for learning and personal growth. Take advantage of retirement to explore new destinations, visit museums, participate in cultural events, and engage with local communities.

- **Stay Curious**: Cultivate a mindset of curiosity and a thirst for knowledge. Explore the world around you with a sense of wonder, and stay open to opportunities for learning and growth in every aspect of your life.

- **Embrace Technology**: Our digital era has made lifelong learning more accessible than ever before. Take advantage of online resources, educational apps, podcasts, and audiobooks to continue learning on the go—anytime and anywhere.

Finding Joy & Fulfillment with Hobbies

Hobbies aren't just pastimes—they're also avenues for self-expression, creativity, and joy. Whether you're passionate about gardening, woodworking, or birdwatching, honing your hobbies in retirement adds richness and meaning to your life.

The following are some ways to rediscover old curiosities or discover new ones:

- **Reflect on Your Interests**: Start by thinking about past activities that have brought you joy or that you've always wanted to pursue. Consider hobbies you enjoyed during your younger years, as well as new interests that you've developed over time.

- **Try New Things**: Retirement gives you time to explore new hobbies and activities that you've never had the chance for previously. Be open to trying new things, whether it's painting, gardening, cooking, photography, playing a musical instrument, or participating in outdoor adventures like hiking or birdwatching.

- **Join Clubs or Groups**: Look for others in your community that cater to your hobbies and interests. Whether it's a knitting circle, a photography club, a hiking group, or a book club, joining like-minded individuals can provide social connections, support, and camaraderie while pursuing your hobbies.

- **Create a Hobby Space**: Designate a dedicated space in your home where you can indulge in your hobbies without distractions. A cozy corner for reading, a studio for painting, or a workshop for woodworking come to mind, but regardless of what strikes you, having a designated hobby space can enhance your enjoyment and focus.

Remember that the joy and fulfillment of hobbies often lie in the process rather than the end result. Embrace the journey of learning, experimenting, and creating, and don't be afraid to make mistakes or try new approaches. Enjoy the contentment that comes from immersing yourself in the activities you love.

You Gotta Have Friends: Building Social Connections

Friends and acquaintances are an integral part of life—especially in retirement. You can forge new connections by joining groups, going to events, volunteering, taking classes, visiting senior centers, hosting gatherings, and staying active in your community. Retirement is also a great opportunity to reconnect with old friends from years gone by. By being open and proactive, you can fight loneliness, enjoy your retirement more, and build a strong support network for a better quality of life.

Maintaining Previous Friendships in Retirement

Retirement doesn't mean saying goodbye to old friends; rather, it's an opportunity to deepen those connections. Make time for regular meetups, phone calls, or video chats to stay connected with loved ones from all the different eras in your life (except for the ones that you'd rather not see again—there's always a few of those!). **Below are several ways to prioritize relationships with friends:**

- **Regular Communication**: Keep in touch through calls, emails, or social media to stay updated on each other's lives.

- **Schedule Reunions**: Plan periodic get-togethers to catch up in person and reminisce about shared memories.

- **Shared Interests**: Engage in activities or hobbies you both enjoy, strengthening your bond through shared experiences.

- **Support Each Other**: Stand by your friends during difficult times, providing them with support and words of encouragement.

- **Celebrate Milestones**: Acknowledge important events in each other's lives, celebrating achievements and milestones together.

- **Flexibility**: Understand that schedules may be busy, so remain flexible in making plans that work for both parties.

- **Group Gatherings**: Organize group events to reconnect with multiple friends, fostering a sense of community.

Volunteering: Creating Connections While Doing Good

Selflessly donating your time offers a meaningful way to create connections while making a positive impact in your community. **Volunteering can foster connections and bring fulfillment in retirement in a number of ways:**

- **Meet New People**: Volunteering introduces you to a diverse range of individuals, including fellow volunteers, staff members, and community members. You'll have the opportunity to create new friendships and build supportive networks.

- **Shared Purpose**: Finding a cause that you care deeply about fosters a sense of purpose, and sharing it with other volunteers strengthens connections, fostering a sense of camaraderie and belonging.

- **Builds Empathy**: Engaging with people from diverse backgrounds promotes open-mindedness and cultivates meaningful connections based on mutual respect and compassion.

- **Social Interaction**: It offers opportunities for social interaction and meaningful engagement. You can enjoy the companionship and camaraderie of fellow volunteers when working on group projects.

- **Skill Sharing**: Leverage your know-how, intellect, and life experiences to make a positive impact through volunteering. Whether mentoring youth, teaching a class, or providing professional expertise, sharing your knowledge with others fosters connections and creates a feeling of fulfillment.

- **Sense of Belonging**: Volunteering builds connections and provides a sense of belonging. Being actively involved in community initiatives and making a difference in the lives of others strengthens ties to the community and enhances overall well-being.

- **Personal Growth**: It offers opportunities to learn new skills, garner valuable experiences, and broaden your horizons. Engaging in meaningful volunteer work promotes a sense of accomplishment and self-worth.

- **Long-Lasting Impact**: Donating your time leaves an enduring impression on both individuals and communities, creating a legacy of service and compassion. The connections forged through volunteering endure beyond retirement, enriching retirees' lives and leaving a positive mark on the world.

Joining Clubs & Organizations: Find Your Tribe

This is a great way to cultivate meaningful connections in retirement. **Here's how becoming involved in clubs and organizations can help you feel a sense of belonging and fulfillment:**

- **Shared Interests**: Clubs and organizations often revolve around specific interests or hobbies, providing you with opportunities to connect with like-minded individuals who share their passions. Whether it's a book club, gardening group, hiking club, or art association, finding a club that aligns with your interests allows you to bond with others who share your enthusiasm.

- **Sense of Community**: Joining a club or organization creates a sense of belonging, providing you with a supportive network of individuals who understand and appreciate your interests and values. Being part of a community fosters friendships, camaraderie, and a sense of shared identity, enriching your social life and general well-being.

- **Opportunities for Socialization**: Clubs and organizations offer regular opportunities for camaraderie and interaction, whether through meetings, events, outings, or group activities. Spend time with fellow club members, engaging in conversations, sharing experiences, and building meaningful relationships.

- **Learning and Growth**: Many groups provide opportunities for personal growth through workshops, guest speakers, or hands-on activities. Pursue activities while connecting with others who share your interests.

- **Sense of Purpose**: Being actively involved in a club or organization gives you a sense of meaning during your retirement. Whether serving in leadership roles, volunteering for committee work, or contributing to group projects, you can make valuable contributions to your community and feel a sense of fulfillment by being part of something larger than yourself.

- **Support and Encouragement**: Social groups can also provide a supportive environment where you can receive encouragement, advice, and support from fellow members. Whether celebrating successes, offering words of encouragement during challenging times, or providing a listening ear, club members often become trusted friends and confidants who offer valuable support and companionship.

- **Opportunities for Leadership**: Joining a club or organization offers you opportunities to take on leadership roles and responsibilities, whether as an officer, committee chair, or event organizer. Serving in leadership positions allows you to develop leadership skills, contribute your expertise, and make a positive impact on your community while forging deeper connections with fellow members.

- **Fun and Enjoyment**: Above all, joining clubs and organizations is about having fun and enjoying life in retirement. Whether participating in group outings, attending social events, or simply spending time with friends who share your interests, you can experience joy, laughter, and fulfillment through your involvement in clubs and organizations.

What Legacy Will You Leave?

This is quite the question. In fact, it's a profound one that prompts you to reflect on the impact you want to have on the world and the lasting imprint you hope to leave behind. This reflection encompasses personal values, contributions to others, professional achievements, nurturing relationships, community involvement, creative expression, teaching and mentorship, and personal growth. By living with intention, purpose, and compassion, you can leave a legacy that reflects your values, passions, and aspirations, inspiring others to follow in your footsteps and make the world a better place.

Charitable Giving in Retirement

As mentioned earlier, giving to charities allows you to help causes you care about, find fulfillment, and leave a lasting legacy. You can support various causes, feel good about your contributions, and potentially receive tax benefits. It also connects you with others and educates your families about giving back. By giving to charities, you make a positive impact and leave a meaningful legacy for the future—all while feeling a sense of contentment and selflessness with yourself at the same time.

Ways to give charitably during your retirement (or anytime, really!) include:

- **Direct Donations**: You can make direct monetary donations to charitable organizations that align with your r values and causes you care about.

- **Donor-Advised Funds**: Establishing one of these allows you to make a contribution to a public charity fund. Save on taxes by setting up a grant for a specific charity that you really care about.

- **Charitable Remainder Trusts**: These allow you to donate assets to a trust while retaining income from those assets during your lifetime. After your passing, the remaining trust assets are distributed to designated charities.

- **Charitable Gift Annuities**: Donate assets to a charitable organization in exchange for a fixed income for life. Upon your passing, the remaining assets go to the designated charity.

- **Legacy Giving**: You can include charitable bequests in your will or estate plan, specifying a portion of your estate to be donated to a charity after you pass on. You'll leave a lasting legacy and support causes that resonated with you during your lifetime.

- **Corporate Matching Programs**: If you're still working, check with your company to see if they match your donations to eligible nonprofit organizations. Some employers offer the same benefit to retirees.

- **Gifts of Appreciated Assets**: You can donate appreciated assets such as real estate, stocks, or bonds directly to organizations, after which you'll receive a tax deduction and avoid capital gains taxes.

- **Charitable IRA Distributions**: Retirees aged 70½ or older can make tax-free charitable donations directly from their IRAs to qualified charitable organizations. These qualified charitable distributions count toward the required minimum distribution and can result in tax savings. [16]

- **Participating in Fundraising Events**: By fundraising or donating to events, you can support its programs and services in a meaningful way, and also make some new friends while you're at it.

Immortal Heirlooms: Passing Down Family Stories & Values

Sharing priceless tales and values from your life with loved ones ensures that your legacy lives on for generations to come. Through storytelling, families can guarantee that their heritage and wisdom will endure and enrich the lives of future generations, thus strengthening family bonds. By passing down these cherished narratives and values, families create lasting connections that transcend time, leaving behind a legacy that's as timeless as it is treasured. **Below are some ways to share your experiences:**

- **Word of Mouth**: Share family stories verbally during family gatherings, meals, or special occasions. Also, encourage older family members to recount their memories and experiences as well, allowing younger generations to listen and learn.

- **Recorded Interviews**: Capture your stories, memories, and insights using audio or video recording equipment to document these interviews, preserving them for future generations to listen to and learn from.

- **Photographs and Documents**: Use old pictures, letters, and other memorabilia to accompany family stories and add visual context. You can also create scrapbooks or digital photo albums that combine images with written narratives to tell your family's story visually.

- **Family Tree**: Create a genealogical chart that documents the relationships between different family members across multiple generations. Include brief biographical details and anecdotes about each individual to add depth and context to the family history. This is an incredible way to fill in the gaps of who's who in the family lineage.

- **Digital Media**: Websites, blogs, or social media are a great place to share family stories and memories. Create a dedicated family website or social media page where family members can contribute stories, photos, and updates.

- **Storytelling Events**: Organize tale-swapping sessions or family reunions where family members can come together to share stories, memories, and experiences. Encourage participation from all generations, fostering intergenerational connections and dialogue.

- **Family Traditions and Rituals**: Incorporate family stories into existing gatherings and celebrations. For example, retell stories about family ancestors during the holidays or incorporate family recipes into special meals, passing down both the food and the stories behind it.

- **Educational Projects**: Encourage younger family members to research and document their family history as part of school projects or educational assignments. Provide guidance and resources to help them explore their roots and discover the richness of their heritage.

- **Digital Storytelling Tools**: Use digital storytelling tools and software to create multimedia presentations or videos that combine audio recordings, photographs, and video clips to tell compelling family stories in a dynamic and engaging format.

Anna is a great example of passing down all the knowledge, stories, and experiences you've amassed during your exciting lifetime. She immigrated to the United States from Russia when she was young and enjoyed a long career traveling the world. Now that she's older, she loves to share her stories with her family and the community. She's explored speaking engagements at local libraries and youth organizations, and she's also pondering writing a book on her experiences. She's amazed by all of the options available to share her story, and she does so every chance she gets.

Memoirs, Mentorship & Meals: Other Legacy Options

When we think of leaving a legacy, we tend to think of our financial assets, but consider the intangible things we can leave behind as well. As mentioned above, storytelling and sharing knowledge and experience are great ways to leave a lasting impression, but there are many other ways to do this as well. **Here are three alternative options:**

- **Memoirs**: Sharing your life experiences, wisdom, and lessons learned through writing memoirs can be a powerful way to leave a legacy. By documenting your personal history, values, and insights, you can pass down your story to future generations and inspire others. Whether you choose to write a book, create a blog, or record audio or video memoirs, your words can have a profound impact on those who come after you. This can also serve a double purpose if you've ever wanted to write a book but never had the time. Now's your chance.

- **Mentorship**: Mentoring others and passing on your knowledge, skills, and expertise is another meaningful way to leave a legacy. Whether you mentor young people in your profession, volunteer as a mentor for at-risk youth, or provide guidance and support to aspiring entrepreneurs, your investment in others can have a ripple effect that lasts for generations. By sharing your experiences and helping others navigate their own paths, you can leave a lasting impact on individuals and communities alike. Also, it just feels so good to impart our wisdom with others—it helps us to feel valued and appreciated.

- **Meals**: Consider establishing a tradition of family meals or hosting regular gatherings with friends and loved ones where you share stories, laughter, and good food. Passing down family recipes, cooking techniques, and culinary traditions can also be a meaningful way to connect with your heritage and leave a lasting legacy that transcends generations.

These alternative legacy options offer opportunities to share your wisdom, values, and passions with others in meaningful ways. Whether it's sharing your wisdom through mentorship, preserving your life story in a memoir, or passing down cherished family recipes, these personal legacies are priceless gifts to future generations.

Key Takeaways

- Retirement offers opportunities for personal growth, fulfillment, and meaningful contribution beyond just relaxation and leisure.

- Prioritize lifelong learning, nurturing social connections, engaging in regular exercise, prioritizing sleep, and maintaining a balanced diet. All these factors are essential for your general well-being during your retirement years.

- Key components of a safe and effective exercise routine in retirement are to start slowly, incorporate resistance training, add balance exercises, and take plenty of time for rest and recovery.

- Rediscovering old hobbies or exploring new interests fosters fulfillment and further enriches your retirement.

- Engaging in charitable giving during retirement enables you to support causes close to your hearts, find fulfillment, and create a lasting legacy.

- Sharing family stories and values ensures that your legacy endures for generations to come.

Chapter 9

Retirement Resources & Tools

"Happy days are here at last, the days of nine to five are passed,
you've worked your life and paid your dues, now you can do just what you choose!"
-Unknown

Have truer words ever been spoken? Doubtful. But while retirement *is* cause for celebration, you need to ensure that you're armed with the appropriate resources and tools in order to navigate the path with clarity.

In this chapter, we'll explore a variety of additional resources and tools that can help you make informed decisions, manage your finances effectively, and achieve your retirement goals.

Essential Reading for Retirement Planning

By exploring the diverse range of resources available, including blogs, websites, financial magazines, and online forums, you'll gain valuable insights and access expert advice, as well as learn from the experiences of others to create a retirement plan that aligns with your goals and aspirations. Whether you're just embarking on your retirement journey or approaching retirement age, the tools highlighted in this chapter offer guidance and support, empowering you to navigate the intricacies of retirement planning with confidence and enthusiasm.

Current Trends: Keeping Up with Blogs & Websites

Online pages dedicated to personal finance and retirement often feature articles, guides, and expert opinions on topics ranging from investment opportunities to tax considerations. By following reputable sources, you'll stay up to date with the latest developments in retirement planning and make informed decisions about your financial future.

There are some fantastic sites out there, but below are three worth following:

- **The Motley Fool** (www.fool.com): Known for its straightforward and actionable advice on investing and personal finance, The Motley Fool offers a wealth of resources specifically tailored to retirement planning. From articles on retirement savings strategies to podcasts featuring expert interviews, this resource provides valuable insights to help you make informed decisions about your financial future.

- **Investopedia** (www.investopedia.com): As a leading source of financial education and information, Investopedia offers a vast library of articles, tutorials, and guides on retirement planning topics. Whether you're looking to learn about retirement savings vehicles, investment strategies, or tax considerations, this site provides comprehensive resources to help you navigate the complexities of retirement planning with confidence.

- **NerdWallet** (www.nerdwallet.com): NerdWallet serves as a reputable source for impartial evaluations and comparisons of financial products and services. Within its retirement planning section, you'll find comprehensive guides, calculators, and expert advice—all aimed at aiding you in making well-informed decisions regarding saving, investing, and planning for your retirement. From retirement account options to Social Security strategies, NerdWallet covers a wide range of topics relevant to retirees and pre-retirees.

Financial Magazines & Journals

For those who prefer in-depth analysis and expert commentary, financial magazines and journals offer valuable insights into retirement planning strategies, market trends, and economic forecasts. Publications such as *Forbes* and *The Wall Street Journal* provide in-depth articles, interviews with industry experts, and analysis of current events that can help you make sound financial decisions and navigate the complexities of retirement planning.

Here are a few other options:

- **Kiplinger's Personal Finance** (www.kiplinger.com): This online magazine is renowned for its practical advice and expert insights on all aspects of personal finance, including retirement planning. Kiplinger's equips you with feature articles, investment selections, and retirement planning manuals, providing actionable insights to maximize your retirement savings and realize your financial goals.

- **Money Magazine** (www.money.com): This resource offers a mix of articles, expert advice, and real-life stories to inspire and inform readers about retirement planning and financial management. Whether you're looking for tips on maximizing your retirement savings or navigating healthcare costs in retirement, Money Magazine provides practical guidance to help you plan for a secure and fulfilling retirement.

- **Barron's** (www.barrons.com): This is a respected publication known for its in-depth analysis of financial markets, investment trends, and economic developments. Its retirement planning section features articles by industry experts, retirement calculators, and retirement-focused investment strategies to help you build and manage a retirement portfolio that meets your long-term financial objectives.

Online Forums: Real-Life Experiences & Advice

One of the most valuable resources for retirees is the wisdom and experiences of others who've already navigated the path to retirement. Online forums and communities centered around retirement planning enable you to engage with peers and exchange insights drawn from their experiences. Whether you're seeking guidance on investment strategies, healthcare options, or lifestyle choices in retirement, online forums provide a supportive and interactive platform for learning and sharing insights.

Here are some to check out:

- **Bogleheads Forum** (www.bogleheads.org): This is a community of investors dedicated to the principles of low-cost investing and passive index fund strategies. With a dedicated section on retirement planning, the forum offers a wealth of real-life experiences, advice, and support from fellow investors and retirees. Whether you're seeking guidance on asset allocation, withdrawal strategies, or Social Security claiming strategies, the Bogleheads Forum provides a supportive and informative platform for discussing retirement planning topics.

- **Reddit Personal Finance** (https://www.reddit.com/r/personalfinance/): This subreddit is a vibrant community where individuals share their personal finance journeys, ask questions, and offer advice on various financial topics, including retirement planning. With thousands of active members and a diverse range of perspectives, Reddit Personal Finance provides a valuable resource for learning about retirement planning strategies, investment options, and tax considerations. Just be aware that while many if not most of the advice is sound, Reddit can attract some users who don't know exactly what they're talking about—they're strangers, after all—so always double check any info you receive (and actually, that goes for any forum you choose to visit).

- **Early Retirement Forum** (www.early-retirement.org/forums): This is a community of individuals who are passionate about achieving financial independence and early retirement. With discussions on topics such as frugal living, investment strategies, and healthcare options in retirement, the forum offers insights and inspiration for those looking to retire early or achieve financial freedom at any age.

Let's consider Marge for a moment. She has a few questions about her retirement options and wonders if her dreams are too far-fetched. She's asked her friends their opinion, but their knowledge is limited. She still has a lot of questions and decides to go on an online forum to see if others have any insights. She ends up with valuable perspectives and even a few new friends, along with new-found confidence as she heads toward retirement.

Must-Have Financial Tools for Retirement

Having the right financial resources at your disposal is essential for making informed decisions, managing your finances effectively, and achieving your retirement goals. In this section, we'll explore must-have financial tools that can help you crunch the numbers, track your spending, manage your investments, and simplify your tax filing process, empowering you to navigate your retirement journey with confidence and clarity.

Retirement Calculators: Crunching the Numbers

These can help you estimate your future financial needs and determine whether you're on track to meet your retirement goals. By inputting information such as your current savings, expected retirement age, and desired lifestyle in retirement, these calculators can provide personalized projections of your retirement income and expenses.

Below are some examples of these handy resources:

- **Vanguard Retirement Nest Egg Calculator** (https://investor.vanguard.com/tools-calculators/retirement-income-calculator): This is a comprehensive tool that helps you estimate your retirement savings needs based on various factors such as age, income, current savings, expected Social Security benefits, and desired retirement lifestyle. Users have the option to input their financial details and preferences, generating customized forecasts of their retirement income and expenditures. The calculator offers insights into your progress toward meeting your retirement objectives and recommends adjustments to your savings strategy if necessary.

- **Empower Retirement Planner** (https://www.empower.com/portfolio-tracking-benefits): This allows users to input their financial information, retirement goals, and risk tolerance to generate a comprehensive retirement plan. It considers factors such as savings rate, investment returns, inflation, Social Security benefits, and healthcare costs to provide users with personalized projections of their retirement income and expenses. You can visualize your retirement plan and make adjustments to your savings and investment strategy to achieve your desired retirement lifestyle.

- **Fidelity's Retirement Score Calculator**
  (https://www.fidelity.com/calculators-tools/fidelity-retirement-score-tool): This resource allows users to input various financial data, including current savings, retirement age, expected Social Security benefits, and desired retirement lifestyle. It provides personalized projections of retirement income and expenses, taking into account inflation and investment returns. You can adjust your savings rate and retirement age to see how different scenarios affect your retirement readiness.

Budgeting Apps to Keep Track of Your Spending

These useful apps present convenient and user-friendly interfaces for tracking your income, expenses, and savings goals in real-time. Through categorizing spending, setting budget limits, and monitoring progress, they aid in pinpointing areas for potential cost reduction, optimizing spending, and attaining financial goals during retirement.

The following are some budgeting apps to check out:

- **Mint** (https://mint.intuit.com/): Mint stands out as a favored budgeting app, consolidating users' income, expenses, and savings goals into a single platform. By linking bank accounts, credit cards, and other financial accounts, Mint automatically categorizes transactions, enables you to set budget limits, and sends alerts for overspending. The app provides visualizations of spending habits, trends, and savings progress, helping you identify areas where you can cut costs and optimize your budget for a comfortable retirement.

- **YNAB (You Need a Budget)**(https://www.ynab.com)**:** YNAB employs a zero-based budgeting methodology, assisting users in assigning every dollar of income to distinct spending categories, savings objectives, and debt repayments. The app syncs with your bank account to import transactions and allows you to categorize spending, set budget limits, and track your progress in real time. YNAB also provides educational materials and support to aid you in adopting sound financial habits.

- **EveryDollar** (https://www.everydollar.com/app): EveryDollar operates as a budgeting app rooted in the zero-based budgeting technique endorsed by financial authority Dave Ramsey. You can create a monthly budget by assigning every dollar of income to specific spending categories such as groceries, housing, and entertainment. The app syncs with your bank account to track expenses in real time and provides visualizations of spending trends and progress toward budget goals. EveryDollar also offers budgeting tips and resources.

Investment Platforms for Managing Your Portfolio

These provide an array of investment opportunities such as stocks, bonds, mutual funds, and ETFs, along with tools and resources for constructing and overseeing a diversified portfolio. Whether you favor a DIY approach or desire professional assistance, these platforms offer the versatility and assistance required for you to make informed investment choices and reach your long-term financial aims. With investment platforms, you gain access to a plethora of investment options, monitor your portfolio's performance, and modify your investment strategy as necessary to navigate shifting market dynamics and fulfill your retirement objectives.

Below are some investment platforms to explore:

- **Fidelity Investments** (www.fidelity.com): Fidelity Investments presents an investment platform featuring an extensive array of investment choices, encompassing stocks, bonds, mutual funds, ETFs, and retirement accounts like IRAs and 401(k)s. You can access Fidelity's online brokerage platform to research investment opportunities, build and manage a diversified portfolio, and monitor your portfolio performance. Fidelity also offers tools and resources, such as retirement planning calculators and educational materials.

- **Charles Schwab** (www.schwab.com): Charles Schwab offers a comprehensive investment platform that includes brokerage accounts, retirement accounts, managed portfolios, and investment advisory services. You'll have the opportunity to explore a broad spectrum of investment choices, spanning stocks, bonds, mutual funds, ETFs, and retirement funds, alongside research tools and educational resources aimed at aiding you in making well-informed investment choices. Charles Schwab also provides retirement planning tools and calculators to help you set and track your retirement goals and manage your portfolio accordingly.

- **TD Ameritrade** (www.tdameritrade.com): TD Ameritrade provides a comprehensive investment platform featuring an extensive array of investment choices, research tools, and educational materials tailored to investors at every stage of learning. You can trade stocks, ETFs, mutual funds, options, and fixed income securities through TD Ameritrade's online brokerage platform. The platform also provides retirement accounts, such as IRAs and 401(k)s, as well as portfolio management services and investment advisory solutions to help you build and manage your retirement portfolio effectively.

Let's see how Meg utilizes the tools available to her. She's been contributing money to her work's 401(k) plan for many years without paying much attention to the balance. Now that she's nearing retirement age, she wonders if she'll have enough to reach her goals or if she should work a few more years. Since her employer's account is managed through Fidelity, she decides to go to their website and use their calculators and financial resources to learn more.

Tax Software: Simplifying Your Tax Filing

Tax software simplifies the tax filing process by guiding you through the necessary steps and helping you identify deductions and credits that can reduce your tax liability. Whether you're filing as an individual or managing complex investment income, tax software streamlines the process and ensures compliance with ever-changing tax laws, allowing you to focus on enjoying your retirement. With tax software, you can file your taxes accurately and efficiently, minimize your tax burden, and maximize your savings for retirement.

- **TurboTax** (www.turbotax.intuit.com/): TurboTax stands out as a premier tax preparation software, streamlining the tax filing journey for individuals, retirees included. You'll answer a series of questions about your income, deductions, and credits, and TurboTax guides you through the necessary steps to complete your tax return accurately. The software offers various versions tailored to different tax situations, such as TurboTax Deluxe for homeowners and TurboTax Premier for investors and rental property owners. TurboTax also provides tools and resources to help you maximize their deductions and credits, file your taxes electronically, and track your refund status.

- **H&R Block Online** (www.hrblock.com): H&R Block offers online tax preparation software. You can input your tax information, deductions, and credits using a step-by-step interview process, and the software guides you through the necessary forms and calculations to complete your tax return accurately. H&R Block also offers additional features such as tax advice from certified tax professionals, audit support, and access to tax planning tools and resources to help you maximize your tax savings and minimize your tax liability.

- **TaxAct** (www.taxact.com): TaxAct is a tax preparation software. You can input your tax information using a step-by-step interview process, with options to import data from previous tax returns or financial institutions. TaxAct provides calculations for various tax scenarios, deductions, and credits, helping you maximize your tax refund or minimize your tax liability. The software also offers additional features such as tax advice, audit support, and tax planning tools to assist you with your tax-related needs.

Government & Nonprofit Resources

There are also valuable resources available from government and nonprofit organizations to help make retirement planning easier. In this section, we'll explore some options that provide information, tools, and support for understanding benefits like Social Security, managing taxes, and protecting consumer rights. By tapping into these resources, you can feel more confident as you navigate the journey toward a secure and fulfilling retirement.

Understanding Your Social Security Benefits

Social Security plays a vital role in retirement income for many Americans, but navigating its intricacies can be challenging. The SSA's official website (https://www.ssa.gov/) offers comprehensive information about Social Security benefits, retirement eligibility, spousal benefits, survivor benefits, and disability benefits. You can access your Social Security statements, estimate your benefits, and learn about the various factors that impact your retirement benefits, such as work history and claiming age.

Helpful IRS Resources with Tax Information for Retirees

The Internal Revenue Service (www.irs.gov) website provides a wealth of tax information and resources for retirees, including tax forms, publications, and FAQs. You can also learn about tax implications for various retirement income sources. In addition, the IRS offers online tools, such as the Interactive Tax Assistant, to help retirees navigate tax-related questions and issues.

Consumer Financial Protection Bureau: Protecting Your Rights

The CFPB offers consumer education resources and tools to help retirees make informed financial decisions and protect their rights. Its website provides information on topics such as retirement planning, managing debt in retirement, avoiding scams and fraud, and understanding financial products and services. You can access guides, worksheets, and interactive tools to help you navigate various financial challenges in retirement.[17]

Support, Education & Advocacy from AARP

AARP is a nonprofit organization dedicated to advocating for the interests of older adults and providing resources and support to help them live their best lives in retirement. It offers a wide range of resources for retirees, including articles, guides, webinars, and workshops on topics such as retirement planning, healthcare, caregiving, and fraud prevention. Members can also access discounts on products and services, as well as community events and volunteer opportunities through local AARP chapters.

Continuing Education Opportunities

Knowledge is power, and continuing education offers opportunities to expand your financial literacy and enhance your retirement strategy. In this section, we'll explore various avenues for ongoing learning, including online courses, community college classes, webinars, podcasts, and financial literacy programs. These resources offer invaluable insights, practical skills, and expert guidance to support you in making informed decisions and reaching your retirement objectives. Whether you favor self-paced online learning or attending in-person workshops (which also advantageously incorporate the social aspect—always helpful in retirement), there are options tailored to accommodate your learning preferences and timetable. Let's uncover the benefits of continuing education in retirement planning and discover how it can empower you to build a secure and fulfilling financial future.

Online Personal Finance Courses

These courses cover a wide range of topics relevant to retirement planning, including budgeting, investing, retirement savings strategies, tax planning, and estate planning. There are classes designed for beginners and for those seeking more technical information. Many online platforms offer interactive lessons, quizzes, and assignments to help you apply what you've learned and track your progress. Online learning is convenient and you can study at your own pace. Whether you're preparing for retirement or simply looking to improve your financial literacy, online personal finance courses provide a valuable opportunity to expand your knowledge and confidence in managing your finances effectively.

The following are just some of the options available:

- **Coursera** (www.coursera.org): Coursera partners with top universities and institutions to offer a wide range of online courses, including personal finance. Courses such as "Personal & Family Financial Planning" by the University of Florida and "Financial Planning for Young Adults" by Purdue University cover topics such as budgeting, saving, investing, and retirement planning.

- **Udemy** (www.udemy.com): Udemy hosts online courses in personal finance. Courses such as "Personal Finance Masterclass: Easy Guide to Better Finances" and "Investing In Stocks The Complete Course! (11 Hour)" provide comprehensive insights into financial management, investment strategies, and retirement planning.

- **edX** (www.edx.org): edX offers courses from leading universities and institutions worldwide, with options for self-paced learning or instructor-led classes. Examples include "Finance for Everyone: Smart Tools for Decision Making" by the University of Michigan and "Retirement Planning: Live Long and Prosper" by RITx.

- **Khan Academy** (www.khanacademy.org): Khan Academy provides free, high-quality educational content on a variety of subjects, including personal finance. Their finance and capital markets section covers topics such as investing, retirement accounts, and taxes, providing a comprehensive overview of key financial concepts.

- **LinkedIn Learning** (www.learning.linkedin.com): LinkedIn Learning offers professional development courses, including personal finance topics. Courses such as "Retirement Planning Foundations" and "Personal Finance Tips Weekly" provide practical insights and strategies for managing finances and planning for retirement.

In-Person Community College Classes

These "real life" courses provide an opportunity for hands-on learning and interaction with instructors and fellow students in a traditional classroom setting. They cover a wide range of personal finance topics, so there's plenty to choose from. If you have a busy schedule, you can check out evening and weekend classes. Additionally, community college classes are typically affordable and may even offer financial aid options for eligible students. By attending in-person community college classes, you can gain valuable knowledge and skills to help you plan for retirement and achieve your financial goals while benefiting from personalized instruction and support from experienced educators. You'll even likely make some new friends along the way.

Learning On the Go with Webinars and Podcasts

These online resources make learning about retirement planning easy and flexible. Webinars are like online seminars in which experts share advice on saving, investing, and taxes. Podcasts, on the other hand, are audio shows that cover similar topics but in a casual, easy-to-understand way, and you can also learn on the go. These resources can help you stay informed about retirement planning without disrupting your routine.

The following are some options to check out:

Webinars

- **Fidelity Webinars** (www.fidelity.com/learning-center/): Fidelity Investments regularly hosts webinars on retirement planning topics such as saving for retirement, Social Security strategies, investment options, and healthcare in retirement. These webinars feature expert speakers and offer practical insights to help you plan for a secure retirement.

- **Vanguard Webcasts** (https://investor.vanguard.com/investor-resources-education): Vanguard offers webcasts on various aspects of retirement planning, including retirement income strategies, investment planning, and tax-efficient investing. These webcasts provide information and guidance on a variety of retirement and investment topics.

Podcasts

- **The Retirement Answer Man** (www.rogerwhitney.com): Presented by certified financial planner Roger Whitney, The Retirement Answer Man podcast dives into a diverse array of retirement planning topics, including Social Security, Medicare, investment strategies, and lifestyle considerations. Each episode provides practical advice and actionable tips aimed at assisting listeners in preparing for a prosperous retirement.

- **Retirement Starts Today Radio** (www.retirementstartstodayradio.com): Hosted by certified financial planner Benjamin Brandt, Retirement Starts Today Radio focuses on retirement planning and financial independence. The podcast covers topics such as retirement income planning, tax strategies, portfolio management, and retirement lifestyle considerations, offering valuable insights and guidance for listeners at all stages of their retirement planning.

Financial Literacy Programs: Enhancing Your Knowledge

These excellent programs help you learn more about managing money, including planning for retirement, investing, budgeting, and dealing with debt. They're offered in the form of workshops or seminars and are available from various sources like government agencies, nonprofits, and financial institutions. By participating, you can improve your financial understanding and make wise decisions about your finances.

Check out these resources:

- **Smart About Money (SAM)** (https://www.nefe.org/initiatives/smart-about-money.aspx): SAM provides complimentary online courses and tools covering a broad spectrum of financial subjects such as budgeting, saving, investing, retirement planning, and debt management. Sponsored by the National Endowment for Financial

Education (NEFE), this program provides valuable resources aimed at enhancing your financial literacy.

- **MyMoney.gov**: MyMoney.gov is a website created by the US government that provides resources and tools to help individuals make informed financial decisions. The site offers information on topics such as managing debt, saving for retirement, buying a home, and protecting against fraud. You'll find interactive tools, calculators, and educational materials.

- **Financial Peace University (FPU)** (https://www.ramseysolutions.com/ramseyplus/financial-peace): FPU is a program created by personal finance expert Dave Ramsey. It offers practical lessons and resources to help you get out of debt, save for the future, and achieve financial freedom. The program covers topics such as budgeting, debt reduction, investing, and retirement planning through in-person classes or online courses.

- **Your Money, Your Goals**: This is a toolkit developed by the Consumer Financial Protection Bureau (CFPB) to help you manage your finances and make informed financial decisions. The toolkit talks about setting goals, budgeting, saving, managing debt, and protecting against financial scams. It includes guides and worksheets, as well as resources for consumers and financial educators.[18]

Key Takeaways

- Retirement planning may seem daunting, but with the right resources and tools, you can approach it with confidence.

- Blogs, websites, financial magazines, and online forums offer valuable insights and advice on retirement planning.

- Keep up with current trends by following reputable sources like The Motley Fool, Investopedia, and NerdWallet.

- Financial magazines and journals provide in-depth analysis and expert commentary on retirement planning strategies.

- Online forums allow you to learn from the experiences of others and seek advice on retirement planning topics.

- Essential financial tools for retirement include retirement calculators, budgeting apps, investment platforms, and tax software.

- Retirement calculators help you estimate your future financial needs and determine if you're on track to meet your goals.

- Budgeting apps can assist with tracking your spending, setting budget limits, and achieving your financial goals in retirement.

- Investment platforms offer a range of tools to help you build and manage your portfolio.

- Tax software simplifies the tax filing process and helps you maximize your savings for retirement.

Final Thoughts

Whether you're 25 or 65, you've likely considered your own retirement and how it might look. In fact, the earlier you start thinking about retirement, the better off you are thanks to the power of compound interest. But no matter where you are in the process, you almost certainly have some questions. Throughout this guidebook, we've provided you with valuable resources that you can tap into anytime to ensure that you're on the right track.

Retirees come from all walks of life. Some of us diligently worked for a corporation for 30 years and retired with a comfortable 401(k) plan, while others built their own business that their leaving as a legacy to their family. Some of us have already set aside funds in an IRA, and some others have a little bit of savings and are going to rely mostly on social security. But no matter what your situation, these chapters have shown you how you can save money on taxes and roll your funds over into different financial instruments that can grow.

You've learned the importance of setting goals when it comes to finances, as well as goals for your life in general. You've also learned that hobbies, social connections, and family play a big part in your retirement plans. Perhaps you're planning on transitioning from the boardroom to the ballroom—attending charity events or enjoying Saturday nights tangoing with your loved one (or maybe even a new special someone). You may be planning on heading off to the workshop or your garage because you *finally* have time to fiddle with creating those wooden rocking horses you've always admired. Or, perhaps, you may be content with simply enjoying time on the green, sinking some putts on Tuesdays instead of on overcrowded Saturdays.

We prompted you to think about all kinds of scenarios: What if you or your spouse become sick? What if you find out that you didn't save enough for retirement? What if you count on selling your house and downsizing but the market is in a downturn? What if the cost of living rises and you need to re-evaluate your budget? Our hope is that you've examined these questions carefully—because no one has a crystal ball.

And because we know that everyone's plans look a little different, we've equipped you with plenty of options. Some of us plan to stay in the same house for the rest of our lives, while others want to travel or downsize into a home with a lot less maintenance.

At this point, you may have a solid idea of your retirement plans, but you may also have a dozen more questions—and the resources provided here are a fantastic starting point. Beyond that? If you have questions regarding your investment account, contract the plan's administrator. If you have specific tax questions, consult a tax attorney or retirement specialist.

Retirement should be the most freeing and fulfilling time in your life. Whether it's pursuing long-held passions, embarking on new adventures, or simply cherishing quality time with loved ones, retirement offers endless possibilities for personal growth and enjoyment. It's a time to savor life's richness and embrace the freedom that comes with financial independence. And now that you're armed with the literacy and know-how to set about planning for your retirement, you can ease into this new chapter of your life with ease, confidence, and enthusiasm.

A Parting Gift

As a way of saying thank you for your purchase, we're offering three FREE downloads that are exclusive to our book readers!

First, the Retirement Planning Checklist, which gives you a step-by-step plan for planning the perfect retirement and making your money last. Second, the Estate Planning Checklist which shows you a step-by-step guide to getting your estate plan in order. And finally, the Retirement Tax Savings Guide, which shows you exactly how to minimize your taxes during retirement (and avoid costly mistakes!).

Inside these bonuses, you'll discover:

- A step-by-step checklist for your retirement plan, so you can maximize your savings and avoid any costly pitfalls.

- An exact checklist for each phase of the estate planning process, so you leave no stone unturned and make sure you're fully prepared to protect your heirs and leave a legacy.

- How to minimize your taxes in retirement so you can preserve wealth, maximize income, and achieve your financial goals.

To download your bonuses, you can go to MonroeMethod.com/retirement-plan **or simply scan the QR code below:**

Can You Do Us a Favor?

Thanks for checking out our book.

We're confident this will help you plan your estate, protect your heirs, and leave a lasting legacy!

Would you take 60 seconds and write a quick blurb about this book on Amazon?

Reviews are the best way for independent authors (like us) to get noticed, sell more books, and spread our message to as many people as possible. We also read every review and use the feedback to write future revisions – and future books, even.

Just navigate to the link below or scan the QR code:

https://mybook.to/retirement-plan

Thank you – we really appreciate your support.

About the Author

Garrett Monroe is a pen name for a team of writers with experience in various industries, like retirement planning, estate planning, entrepreneurship, sales, AI, real estate, accounting, etc. They've built teams, gone through the ins and outs of retirement, and know how to properly plan an estate. These writers have come together to share their knowledge and produce a series of books to help you retire well, plan your estate, and protect your loved ones for generations to come.

References

[1] AARP (https://www.aarp.org/)

[2] Starting Your Benefits Early (n.d.). *Social Security Administration* (https://www.ssa.gov/benefits/retirement/planner/agereduction.html).

[3] Current Inflation Rates 2000-2024 (n.d.). *US Inflation Calculator.* (https://www.usinflationcalculator.com/inflation/current-inflation-rates/)

[4] 401(k) limit increases to $23,000 for 2024, IRA limit rises to $7,000 (2023, November 10). *Internal Revenue Service* https://www.irs.gov/newsroom/401k-limit-increases-to-23000-for-2024-ira-limit-rises-to-7000

[5] Plan with Confidence. Partner with a CFP Professional (n.d.). *CFP.* https://www.letsmakeaplan.org/find-a-cfp-professional

[6] Avoiding Retirement Fraud (n.d.). *Investor - US Securities and Exchange Commission.* https://www.investor.gov/additional-resources/retirement-toolkit/avoiding-retirement-fraud

[7] Retirement plan and IRA Requirements FAQ (n.d.). *Internal Revenue Service.* https://www.irs.gov/retirement-plans/retirement-plan-and-ira-required-minimum-distributions-faqs

[8] Setting Every Community Up for Retirement Enhancement Act of 2019 (SECURE Act) (n.d.). *US Department of Labor.*

https://www.dol.gov/agencies/ebsa/laws-and-regulations/laws/secure-act

[9] Getting Started with Medicare (n.d.) *Medicare.gov.* https://www.medicare.gov/basics/get-started-with-medicare

[10] Best Long-term Insurance Care of 2024 (n.d.). *Consumers Advocate.* https://www.consumersadvocate.org/long-term-care-insurance/lp/best-long-term-care-insurance

[11] Kiger, P. (2024, January 25). Retiring in Mexico: What You Need to Know. *AARP.* https://www.aarp.org/retirement/planning-for-retirement/info-2022/retiring-in-mexico.html

[12] Reverse Mortgages (n.d.). *Federal Trade Commission Consumer Advice.* https://consumer.ftc.gov/articles/reverse-mortgages

[13] Stanley, M (2024, April 8) Senior Discounts and Savings. *SeniorLiving.org.* https://www.seniorliving.org/finance/senior-discounts/

[14] Jackson, L (2023, August 21) Estate Planning Guide and Checklist for 2024. *National Council on Aging.* https://www.ncoa.org/adviser/estate-planning/estate-planning-guide-checklist/

[15] National Institute on Aging https://www.nia.nih.gov/

[16] Donating an IRA and other retirement assets (n.d.). *Fidelity Charitable.* https://www.fidelitycharitable.org/guidance/philanthropy/donating-retirement-assets-to-charity.html

[17] Consumer Financial Protection Bureau. https://www.consumerfinance.gov/

[18] Your Money, Your Goals (n.d.) *Consumer Finance.* https://www.consumerfinance.gov/consumer-tools/educator-tools/your-money-your-goals/

Made in United States
Orlando, FL
24 October 2024

52925438R00098